PHILOSOPHICAL ETHICS:
THEORY AND PRACTICE

John G. Messerly, PhD

Copyright © 2015 John G Messerly

All rights reserved.

ISBN: 098882244X

ISBN-13: 978-0-9888224-4-3

Dedication

To Jane, "a lily among the thistles."
Song of Solomon 2:2

PREFACE V

CHAPTER 1 – WHAT IS PHILOSOPHY? 1
1. The Beginnings of Rationalistic Thinking 1
2. Philosophy's Domain 4
3. Philosophy, Science, and Religion 6
4. The Value of Philosophy 8
5. What is Philosophical Ethics? 12
6. The Moral and the Legal 12
7. Moral Theories and Intuitions 13
8. Methodology 15

CHAPTER 2 – IMPEDIMENTS TO ETHICAL THEORY 17
1. Nihilism 17
2. Determinism 18
3. Responses to Determinism 21
4. Psychological Egoism 22
5. Ethical Egoism 24
6. Hedonism 26

CHAPTER 3 – CULTURAL MORAL RELATIVISM 28
1. What is Relativism? 28
2. Critique of Relativism 30
3. Relativism, the Unknown, and Belief 32
4. Summary of Relativism 32
5. What is Cultural Moral Relativism? 34
6. Critique of Cultural Moral Relativism – Part 1 36
7. Critique of Cultural Moral Relativism – Part 2 38

CHAPTER 4 – PERSONAL MORAL RELATIVISM 40
1. What is Personal Moral Relativism? 40
2. Critique of Personal Relativism 41
3. Tolerance and Relativism 43
4. Emotivism 44
5. Critique of Emotivism 46
6. Conclusion 48

CHAPTER 5 – NATURAL LAW THEORY 49

1. The Divine Command Theory 49
2. Plato's Question 50
3. The History of Natural Law Ethics 52
4. St. Thomas Aquinas 54
5. Some Philosophical Difficulties 56
6. Final thoughts 57

CHAPTER 6 - THE SOCIAL CONTRACT 59

1. Hobbes and the Social Contract 59
2. A Theory of Morality 61
3. An Actual Contract 62
4. Morals By Agreement 64
5. Game Theory and the Prisoner's Dilemma 66
6. How Strong is Contract Theory? 69
7. A Veil of Ignorance 71
8. Conclusion 74

CHAPTER 7 – KANT'S ETHICS 76

1. Kant and Hume 76
2. Freedom and Rationality 78
3. Intention, Duty, and Consequences 79
4. Hypothetical and Categorical Imperatives 80
5. Kant's Examples 83
6. Problems with Universalization 86
7. General Difficulties 88
8. Kant's Fundamental Idea 89
9. Conclusion 91

CHAPTER 8 - UTILITARIANISM 92

1. Utility and Happiness 92
2. The Consequences 94
3. Examples of Utilitarian Reasoning 96
4. Mill and Utilitarianism 98

5. ACT AND RULE UTILITARIANISM 100
6. THE PROBLEMS WITH HAPPINESS 102
7. THE PROBLEM WITH CONSEQUENCES 105
8. THE PROBLEMS WITH RULE UTILITARIANISM 106
9. CONCLUSION 108

CHAPTER 9 – EXISTENTIALISM 110

1. BASIC IDEAS OF EXISTENTIALISM 110
2. SARTRE AND FREEDOM 113
3. ANGST, BAD FAITH, AND AUTHENTICITY 115
4. PROBLEMS FOR AN EXISTENTIAL ETHICS 117
5. OTHER EXISTENTIAL THINKERS 119
6. AN ASSESSMENT 121

CHAPTER 10 – EVOLUTION AND ETHICS 123

1. DARWIN AND EVOLUTION 123
2. EVOLUTION AND ETHICS 125
3. SOCIAL DARWINISM 126
4. EVOLUTION AND ETHICS OPPOSED 127
5. EVOLUTION AND ETHICS CONJOINED 129
6. ETHICS AND SOCIOBIOLOGY 130
7. CRITICS OF SOCIOBIOLOGY 133
8. PROBLEMS FOR EVOLUTIONARY ETHICS 135

CHAPTER 11 – ABORTION 137

1. BIOLOGICAL HUMANS ARE PEOPLE 137
2. ABORTION IS IMMORAL 139
3. A DEFENSE OF ABORTION 141
4. FETUSES AREN'T PEOPLE 146
5. CHRISTIANITY AND ABORTION 148
6. AMERICAN POLITICS AND ABORTION 150

CHAPTER 12 – EUTHANASIA AND BIOTECHNOLOGY 152

1. THE EUTHANASIA DEBATE 152
2. EUTHANASIA IS WRONG 153
3. ACTIVE AND PASSIVE EUTHANASIA 155

4. Voluntary Active Euthanasia 156
5. David Hume on Suicide 158
6. Worse Off Alive 160
7. Against the Use of Biotechnology 163
8. In Defense of Cloning Humans 164
9. Against Genetic Engineering 168

CHAPTER 13 – DEATH 171

1. Is Death Bad For Us? 171
2. Death Is Bad For Us 174
3. How Science May Defeat Death 176
4. Death Should Be Optional 179

CHAPTER 14 – THE UNIMAGINABLE FUTURE 187

1. What Would Life Be Like Inside a Computer? 187
2. Would Immortality Be Boring? 189
3. Can "We" Really Live in the Future? 191
4. The Overpopulation Objection 193

CHAPTER 15 – THE MEANING OF LIFE 198

1. The Search for Meaning 198
2. The Question and the Answers 200
3. Cosmic Evolution and the Meaning of Life 203
4. The Meaning of Life Explained 207
5. Final Thoughts 211

Preface

This book grew from my experience teaching ethics courses for almost 30 years. In that time I have taught over 100 sections of college ethics courses including: ethical theory; ethical problems, bioethics; and computer ethics. In this book, I outline the basics of ethical theory as objectively as I can.

I admit to being less objective about the moral issues discussed. I am a non-apologetic transhumanist who believes that we should overcome all human limitations, defeat death, and become post-humans. Hopefully, my arguments will be convincing.

As a teacher, my advice to students is to work hard and lift the mental weights that leads to strong minds. Thinking carefully is something you develop a taste for; but the better you think, the better your chances of living well. As Blaise Pascal put it: "Our whole dignity consists in thought. Let us endeavor, then, to think well: this is the principle of ethics."

My other piece of advice as a teacher comes from Walt Whitman.

> I tramp a perpetual journey, (come listen all!)
> My signs are a rain-proof coat, good shoes, and a staff cut from the woods,
> No friend of mine takes his ease in my chair,
> I have no chair, no church, no philosophy,
> I lead no man to a dinner-table, library, exchange,
> But each man and each woman of you I lead upon a knoll,
> My left hand hooking you round the waist,
> My right hand pointing to landscapes of continents and the public road.
> Not I, not anyone else can travel that road for you,
> You must travel it for yourself.

Chapter 1 – What is Philosophy?

Our whole dignity consists in thought. Let us endeavor, then, to think well: this is the principle of ethics. ~ Blaise Pascal, Pensées, II, 1670

1. The Beginnings of Rationalistic Thinking

The word philosophy comes from two Greek roots meaning "the love of wisdom." Thus philosophers are (supposed to be) lovers of wisdom. In the western world, philosophy traces its beginnings to the ancient Ionian city of Miletus, the richest city in the ancient Greek world. There, on the eastern edge of the Mediterranean in the sixth century B.C.E., the Greeks began to systematically apply human reason to questions concerning nature and human life *without* reference to the supernatural.

The first Greek philosophers were interested in the question "what is the world made of?" Thales (c.585 B.C.E.), the father of Western philosophy, argued that the earth was made of water, although his successors rejected his argument. How, they wondered, could cool and wet water be the basis of hot and dry things? What's important for our purposes isn't the specifics of these arguments, but that for the first time in recorded history hypotheses were being advanced which were subject to rational criticism.

Subsequent thinkers maintained that physical reality was composed of a boundless (Anaximander), air (Anaximenes), fire (Heraclitus), the four elements (Empedocles), or an infinite number of seeds (Anaxagoras). Both monism—the view that one kind of thing comprises reality—and pluralism—that many types of stuff comprise reality—encountered difficulties. Monism couldn't account for plurality, and pluralism couldn't account for unity.

Greek thinking about the nature of the physical world culminated with Democritus (460-360 B.C.E.) and other Greek atomists, who argued that all of reality was made up of empty space and tiny, solid, indestructible atoms. This theory provided a theoretical solution to "the problem of the one and the many," by postulating a qualitative singularity and a quantitative plurality. Material things were identical regarding the qualitative nature of their atoms but differed in the number and configuration of those atoms.

This theory also resolved the "problem of change," the paradox of how something changes into something else and yet remains the same. To understand this problem, consider the following. How are you now both the same person and a different person from when you were a small child? If you are the same, then you aren't different; and if you are different, then you aren't the same. In answer to this conundrum, Heraclitus (c. 500 B.C.E.) proposed that everything constantly changes. Parmenides (c. 515 – 450), on the other hand, asserted that permanence was the fundamental reality, and he used Zeno's famous arguments against the possibility of motion to support his views.

Zeno (c.490-430) had argued that the swift Achilles could never pass a front-running tortoise in a race because, by the time Achilles reached the place where the tortoise was previously, the tortoise would have moved ahead to some further point. When Achilles reached that point, the tortoise would have moved further on again, ad infinitum. So Achilles could never pass the tortoise and motion, a kind of change, was impossible. However, because we ordinarily assume motion is possible, the atomists and pluralists rejected the views of Parmenides and Zeno.

The Atomists argued that atomic transformations account for our perception of change. In reality the number and configurations of atoms changes, but their underlying qualities don't. What we

Chapter 1 – What is Philosophy?

perceive as change is, in fact, quantitative transformation at the atomic level. In little more than a century, rational discourse alone, without the benefit of experimentation, had advanced the argument remarkably.

But atomic theory wasn't the only achievement of Greek rationalism. As Greek influenced spread throughout the Mediterranean over the next few centuries, its accomplishments were most impressive. Hipparchus mapped the constellations and calculated the brightness of stars, and Euclid produced the first systematic geometry. Herophilus argued that the brain was the foundation of intelligence, and Heron invented gear trains and steam engines. Eratosthenes calculated the circumference of the earth with surprising accuracy, mapped the earth, and argued that the Indies could be reached by sailing west. (Yes, ancient scholars knew the earth was round.) Moreover, the accomplishments of Pythagoras the mathematician, Archimedes the mechanical genius, Ptolemy the astronomer, and Hippocrates the physician are legendary.

In Alexandria, where over the course of seven centuries the rationalist spirit flourished, the great library and museum held much of the knowledge of the ancient world. But this rationalistic spirit never seized the imagination of the masses and, in 415 C.E., the mob burned the library down. At the time, the greatest mathematician, scientist and philosopher at work in the library was a woman named Hypatia (c.370 – 415).

Unfortunately, Alexandria in Hypatia's time was in disarray. Roman civilization was in decline and the Catholic Church was growing in power. Cyril, the archbishop of Alexandria, despised Hypatia because of her friendship with the Roman governor and her place as a symbol of rationalism and paganism. On her way to work in 415 C.E., she was met by a fanatical mob of Cyril's parishioners. In his book *Cosmos*, Carl Sagan describes the scene thus: "They dragged her from her chariot, tore off her clothes, and, armed with abalone shells, flayed her flesh from her bones. Her remains were burned, her works obliterated, her name forgotten. Cyril was made a saint."

Though the pursuit of knowledge continued in the Middle East and in Eastern civilization, Western civilization would soon plunge into the dark ages and await the Renaissance, more than a millennium in the distant future, for the rebirth of the rationalistic spirit which began in ancient Greece. We can only speculate as to the increased extent of our scientific knowledge today had the spirit of this investigation continued unabated.

2. Philosophy's Domain

The ancient Greeks made no distinction between rational, philosophical, and scientific thinking. When Thales or Democritus practiced what we would today call physics or chemistry, these disciplines were still *parts* of philosophy. As the centuries proceeded and human reasoned discovered more about various branches of knowledge, the sciences formed their own distinct disciplines. However, this is a relatively recent phenomenon. Newton, for example, considered his revolutionary seventeenth-century work in physics to be *natural philosophy*. The natural sciences as distinct disciplines are recent, and the social sciences even more so. For example, economics and became an independent discipline in (roughly) the early nineteenth century, psychology in the late nineteenth and early twentieth century, and sociology in the early twentieth century.

Today, in the colleges and universities of the Western world, the residual, unanswered, and timeless questions which don't fall within the specific purview of other disciplines comprise

Chapter 1 – What is Philosophy?

philosophy's domain. Therefore some of the most difficult questions, for which there are as yet no definite answers or methodology, remain for philosophers to ponder. For example: Is the belief in a God reasonable? What is knowledge? Do we know anything for certain? What is the ultimate nature of reality? Why is there something rather than nothing? What is the nature of goodness, beauty, truth, liberty, equality, and justice? What is a good political system or fair economic system? What is valuable in art, music, or human conduct? What is morality? Are humans free? What is the meaning of science? What is the relationship between thought and reality? What is language? Are human beings entirely material? What is the meaning and purpose of human existence? These are just a sample of philosophical questions.

Most of these questions fall into a few basic groups. *Metaphysics* probes the nature of ultimate reality and revolves around the question, "what is real?" *Epistemology* studies the nature and limits of human knowledge and centers on the question, "what can we know?" *Axiology* explores the nature of the valuable in art, politics, and ethics and asks, "What is good?" And, since philosophy invokes reasoned arguments to support positions—rather than relying on faith, authority, tradition, or conventions—*logic* is that branch of philosophy that differentiates good arguments from bad ones.

In addition, many specialized fields exist within philosophy. There is philosophy of religion, mathematics, science, law, medicine, business, language, art, sport, and more. Note, one can *practice* any of these without philosophizing about them. You can be a cleric, mathematician, scientist, lawyer, nurse, physician, business executive, linguist, artist or athlete *without* philosophizing about them. So philosophy is by nature a theoretical pursuit rather than a practical one. Philosophers ask: how do we know a religious claim is true? Does mathematics tell us about reality, or is it merely an arbitrary formal system? How do we know scientific theories are true? What justifies the use of legal coercion? What should the practice of medicine entail? Are ethical behaviors and profitable business compatible? Does language effectively communicate ideas? What makes good art? What purpose do sports serve? Any important part of human culture, the culture as a whole, or the ultimate nature of reality itself is ripe for analysis. Thus, *philosophy is sustained, rational, and systematic reflection and analysis of the philosophical area in question.*

In addition, philosophers investigate the relationship between, for example, philosophy and psychology, literature, culture, gender, or history. Is philosophy independent of these forces, or does philosophy depend on them? Philosophers might study the history of philosophy in order to understand the evolution of ideas in history, or they might be more interested in the meaning of human history. Philosophers are also interested in theoretical issues in game theory, decision theory, and cognitive science, as well as practical issues concerning business, medical, and environmental ethics. The range of philosophy is enormous.

For the uninitiated, in order to get a grasp of the nature of philosophy, go into any library or bookstore and examine a work of non-fiction. Often, at the end of the work in question, one finds a section entitled "Afterthoughts," "Reflections," "Postscript," "Epilogue," "What It All Means," etc. There authors often move from their subject matter to reflect on the *meaning* or *implications* of their investigation. At that point, they are philosophizing.

3. Philosophy, Science, and Religion

In order to more clearly conceptualize philosophy's territory, let's consider it in relation to two other powerful cultural forces with which it's intertwined: religion and science. We may

Chapter 1 – What is Philosophy?

(roughly) characterize the contrast between philosophy and religion as follows: *philosophy relies on reason, evidence, and experience for its truths; religion depends on faith, authority grace, and revelation for truth.* Of course, any philosophical position probably contains some element of faith, inasmuch as reasoning rarely gives conclusive proof; and religious beliefs often contain some rational support, since few religious persons rely completely on faith.

The problem of the demarcation between the two is made more difficult by the fact that different philosophies and religions—and philosophers and religious persons within similar traditions—place dissimilar emphasis on the role of rational argument. For example, Eastern religions traditionally place less emphasis on the role of rational arguments than do Western religions, and in the east philosophy and religion are virtually indistinguishable. In addition, individuals in a given tradition differ in the emphasis they place on the relative importance of reason and faith. So the difference between philosophy and religion is one of emphasis and degree. Still, we reiterate what we said above: religion is that part of the human experience whose beliefs and practices rely significantly on faith, grace, authority, or revelation. Philosophy gives little if any, place to these parts of human experience. While religion generally stresses faith and trust, philosophy honors reason and doubt.

Distinguishing philosophy from science is equally difficult because many of the questions vital to philosophers—like the cause and origin of the universe or a conception of human nature— increasingly have been taken over by cosmologists, astrophysicists, and biologists. Perhaps methodology best distinguishes the two, since philosophy relies on argument and analysis rather than empirical observation and experiment. In this way, philosophy resembles theoretical mathematics more than the natural sciences.

Still, philosophers utilize evidence derived from the sciences to reformulate their theories.

Remember also that, until the nineteenth century, virtually every prominent philosopher in the history of western civilization was either a scientist or mathematician. In general, we contend that *science explores areas where a generally accepted body of information and methodology directs research involved with unanswered scientific questions.* Philosophers explore philosophical questions *without* a generally accepted body of information

Philosophical analysis also ponders the future relationship between these domains. Since the seventeenth-century scientific revolution, science has increasingly expropriated territory once the exclusive province of both philosophy and religion. Will the relentless march of science continue to fill the gaps in human knowledge, leaving less room for the poetic, the mystical, the religious, and the philosophical? Will religion and philosophy be archaic, antiquated, obsolete, and outdated? Or will there always be questions of meaning and purposes that can never be grasped by science? Bertrand Russell (1872-1970), one of the twentieth century's greatest philosophers, elucidated the relationship between these three domains like this: "All *definite* knowledge ... belongs to science; all dogma as to what surpasses definite knowledge belongs to theology. But between theology and science there is a no man's land, exposed to attack from both sides; this no man's land is philosophy."

4. The Value of Philosophy

What is the value of philosophy? To this question, we propose some possible answers. First, it's *natural* to wonder, to ask questions. Children are marvelous philosophers who never tire of asking questions. However, you may reply that nature doesn't necessitate duty and that you don't find it natural to philosophize. Second, philosophizing is *pleasurable*. We find great joy asking questions and considering possibilities. Perhaps that is why Plato called philosophizing "that dear delight." Nonetheless, you might counter that it doesn't suit your tastes. Third, we appeal to philosophy's *usefulness*. Any kind of knowledge is potentially useful, and if philosophy engenders a bit of knowledge and wisdom, then it's worthwhile. Nevertheless, you may not value either wisdom or knowledge unless it engenders material reward.

Finally, we argue that philosophy *protects* us against unsupported ideology, unjustified authority, unfounded beliefs, baseless propaganda, and questionable cultural values. These forces may manipulate us if we don't understand them and can't think critically about them. This doesn't require a *rejection* of cultural values, only a reflection upon them. Otherwise, they aren't *our* values, ideas, or beliefs—we have accepted them second-hand. To this you might respond that reflection is laborious, that ignorance is bliss, and that trust in authority and tradition maintain the continuity of culture.

Therefore you could conceivably reject all of our arguments. In the absence of definitive arguments, individuals must decide whether philosophy is a worthwhile pursuit. We all decide whether the pursuit of wisdom, knowledge, wealth, fame, pleasure or anything else is worth the effort. In the end, to value philosophy we must believe that reflection, questioning, contemplation, and wonder enrich human life; we must believe with Socrates that "the unexamined life isn't worth living." I believe that a life without reflection is hardly worth living.

Questions about the value of philosophy entwine with issues concerning education. What is the point of education? Is it merely to learn practical techniques? Consider a nurse or physician who has mastered all of the techniques necessary to practice their professions. Are they complete nurses or physicians? Most of us would say no; they need to understand the persons they treat holistically, and this knowledge doesn't come merely from their technical training. Thus, we do recognize the place in our education for philosophy, literature, poetry, psychology, and history even though they may not be *practical*. However, if material needs are all that matter, then the life of the mind may be irrelevant.

But imagine instead that education increases our awareness, diminishes our dogmatism, and enables us to be capable of happiness and wisdom. Is the point of lifting weights merely to push them against the force exerted by gravity? No! We seek instead to transform our physiques, accomplish our goals, learn the valuable lesson that nothing comes without effort and that life's greatest joys accompany personal struggle and subsequent triumph. And through this process, our bodies are literally transformed. Analogously, education transforms us in a more fundamental way. Jiddu Krishnamurti stated the case as follows:

> Why do we go through the struggle to be educated? Is it merely in order to pass some examinations and get a job? Or is it the function of education to prepare us while we are young to understand the whole process of life? Surely, life isn't merely a job, an occupation: life is wide and profound, it's a great mystery, a vast realm in which we function as human beings.

In this context Russell, in *The Problems of Philosophy*, wrote:

> The [person] who has no tincture of philosophy goes through life imprisoned in the prejudices derived from

Chapter 1 – What is Philosophy?

> common sense, from the habitual beliefs of [their] age or [their] nation, and from convictions which have grown up in [their] mind without the cooperation or consent of [their] deliberate reason. To such a [person] the world tends to become definite, finite, obvious; common objects rouse no questions, and unfamiliar possibilities are contemptuously rejected. As soon as we begin to philosophize, on the contrary, we find… that even the most everyday things lead to problems to which only very incomplete answers can be given. Philosophy…. removes the somewhat arrogant dogmatism of those who have never traveled into the region of liberating doubt…

Finally, consider the view of the great twentieth-century historian and philosopher Will Durant, who in the preface to *The Mansions of Philosophy* said this about the purpose of philosophy:

> Philosophy will not fatten our purses…For what if we should fatten our purses, or rise to high office, and yet all the while remain ignorantly naïve, coarsely unfurnished in the mind, brutal in behavior, unstable in character, chaotic in desire, and blindly miserable?

> Our culture is superficial today, and our knowledge dangerous, because we are rich in mechanisms and poor in purposes … We move about the earth with unprecedented speed, but we don't know, and haven't thought, where we are going, or whether we shall find any happiness there for our harassed souls. We are being destroyed by our knowledge, which has made us drunk with our power. And we shall not be saved without wisdom.

5. What is Philosophical Ethics?

Ethics is that part of philosophy which deals with the good and bad, or right and wrong, in human conduct. It asks: What is the good? What should I do? What is a good life? Is morality objective or subjective? Is it absolute or relative? Why should I be moral? What is the relationship between self-interest and morality? Where does morality come from? What, if anything, provides the ultimate justification for morality? Should one emphasize duty, happiness, or pleasure in moral judgments? Traditionally, ethicists sought to give general advice on how to live a good and happy life, but contemporary philosophers have increasingly moved to more abstract and theoretical questions. While some contemporary philosophers have voiced alarm at this trend, many contemporary ethicists still ask esoteric questions.

We may conveniently divide contemporary philosophical ethics into at least four parts. *Meta-ethics* conducts an analysis of moral concepts, ethical justification, and the meaning of moral language. *Descriptive ethics* describes ethical behavior among various people and in various cultures. (Social scientists now do most of this work.) *Normative ethics* contemplates the norms, standards, or criteria that serve as theories or principles of ethical behavior. *Applied ethics* applies normative theories to particular ethical problems like abortion, euthanasia, capital punishment, sexuality etc. Some areas of applied ethics have become their own sub-specialties like medical, environmental, business, or computer ethics.

6. The Moral and the Legal

It's especially important to differentiate morality and law, inasmuch as discussion of the moral and legal often conflate. On the one hand, the two differ since we believe some legal acts to be immoral, and some laws to be unjust. And even if the law didn't prohibit murder, stealing, and the like, we would probably still consider them wrong. This suggests that the two aren't co-extensive. On the other hand, the two are connected because the law embodies many moral precepts. Legal prohibitions incorporate most of our ordinary moral rules such as those against lying, killing, cheating, raping, and stealing. This suggests there is some connection between the moral and the legal.

Though it's possible to have morality without law, or law without morality, the two usually go together. Therefore, we suggest that law codifies morality. In other words, the law formulates the culture's morality into legal codes. Again, not every legal code refers to a moral issue, but most laws do have some moral significance. Though a connection between the moral and legal exists, they clearly aren't the same things.

While a thing's illegality may give us a reason not to do the thing, this is a prudential rather than moral reason. In other words, if we are afraid to steal because we might get caught, then we fear punishment, not immorality. Nevertheless, we might offer moral reasons to abide by the law. We could say that we owe it to the state to abide by their laws and that civil disobedience undermines both the moral fabric and our tacit agreement with the state. This was essentially Socrates' argument against escaping from Athens before his impending execution. But in general, legal arguments aren't applicable to ethical discussion. Ethicists generally discuss morality, not legality, as will we.

7. Moral Theories and Intuitions

The moral theories we encounter in this book often conflict with our moral intuitions; they are often counter-intuitive. Explanations, theories, or beliefs are counter-intuitive if they violate our ordinary, common-sense view. For example, it's counter-intuitive to suppose that physical reality is illusory, although there is no way to demonstrate this isn't the case. Similarly, it's counter-intuitive to suppose the keyboard upon which I type is moving, although the keyboard, earth, solar system, galaxy, and entire universe move! This demonstrates that non-moral intuitions are often mistaken.

Surely our moral intuitions are sometimes wrong too. To see this point, consider some moral beliefs and practices once thought to be consistent with our moral intuitions: human slavery; the inferiority of women; human sacrifice; debtor's prisons; dueling; torture; witch burning; etc. Since most of us now believe these practices are wrong, we must admit that our former moral intuitions were mistaken. But isn't it possible that many of our present moral intuitions will be rejected in the future? For instance, can we not imagine that in the future meat-eating or solitary confinement will be thought barbaric? And if we reject a present intuition at some later date, then they aren't sacrosanct now.

Thus the mere fact that a theory violates our moral intuitions isn't necessarily a reason to reject the theory; we might reject our intuitions instead. How do we resolve the dispute between the two? One of the ways of resolving the dispute between moral intuitions and moral theories is to achieve what contemporary philosophers call *reflective equilibrium*, which calls for a balance between moral intuitions and theories. If a theory radically contradicts our moral intuitions, then the theory should probably be rejected. On the other hand, id the theory has a number of explanatory advantages and only slightly challenges our moral intuition, then the intuition should probably be rejected.

But most classic moral theories aren't generally counter-intuitive. In fact, they are classic because they explain so much of our ordinary moral consciousness. Nonetheless, since no theory is perfect, almost any proposed moral theory generates some counter-intuitive results. Perhaps this reveals to each of us, that we don't have a *privileged moral status*. If our moral status were privileged, then we could measure any proposed theory against it. But we will assume that our moral status and intuitions aren't privileged. They don't provide unique insight into moral truth. If our moral status were privileged this investigation would be irrelevant, since we would already possess moral truth. We reject this claim.

The same issue applies when we turn from explaining morality to justifying it. Contemporary philosophers offer three basic kinds of justification for morality. Some, following Plato and Hobbes, argue that morality is based in self-interest. Others, following Hume and Mill, suggest that morality rests upon some sentiments, emotions, or sympathies we happen to have. Others, following Kant, insist that morality is grounded in reason. In addition to these philosophical justifications, some metaphysicians and theologians maintain that the source of morality rests in the metaphysical order. Whatever our moral intuitions about moral justification, we assume that these intuitions aren't privileged.

8. Methodology

I try to investigate various moral theories as objectively as possible. Yet we might remember that treating all theories as equally true doesn't mean they are equally true. Easily confused is the assumption that because there are two sides to every story both of those sides are equally true. One side may say the earth is round, billions of years old, home to evolving species, and undergoing climate change; while the other says the earth is flat, a few thousands of years old, with fixed species, and the climate not changing, But one of these sides is wrong!

Of course, it's tedious to carefully and conscientiously examine ideas, especially ones that we favor. We desperately cling to believing exactly what we now believe because belief is a tranquil state. But to truly become our own thinkers, and not merely to accept those ideas with which we have been indoctrinated, we must think for ourselves. As the motto of the Enlightenment says, dare to think! It's difficult to think well, but in the process of an intellectual journey we are transformed, no matter how difficult it might be. As Spinoza noted long ago on the final page of his 1677 work *Ethics Demonstrated in the Geometric Manner*:

> If the way which, as I have shown, leads hither seems very difficult, it can nevertheless be found. It must indeed be difficult, since it's so seldom discovered, for if salvation lay ready to hand and could be discovered without great labour, how could it be possible that it should be neglected almost by everybody? But all noble things are as difficult as they are rare.

Chapter 2 – Impediments to Ethical Theory

I don't know how to teach philosophy without becoming a disturber of the peace. ~ Baruch Spinoza

1. Nihilism

The word nihilism derives from the Latin nihil meaning "nothing" and refers variously to: 1) the denial of any basis of knowledge; 2) the general rejection of conventional morality or religion; 3) the doctrine that social progress can be achieved only by the destruction of social and political organizations; or 4) the general belief that life is without meaning or purpose. *Ethical nihilism* denies the validity of all moral distinctions; thus, helping an elderly woman across the street doesn't differ morally from stealing her purse. To put it more bluntly, the nihilist finds nothing wrong with killing your mother!

Ethical nihilism is counter-intuitive. As we saw before, a doctrine is counter-intuitive if it offers a fundamental challenge to any strongly held moral intuition or belief. For example, if I claimed that a deity rewards the wicked and punishes the virtuous, you would likely reject the doctrine as counter-intuitive. Analogously, we reject ethical nihilism because it *strongly* contradicts our ordinary moral intuitions. Of course, as we said before, the fact that some idea conflicts with our intuition doesn't mean that idea is wrong. So it would take a lot more than an appeal to the counter-intuitive to mount a full case against moral nihilism.

Still, ethical nihilism denies the possibility of an enterprise woven into the fabric of human intellectual history, and of the utmost practical importance. So without compelling reasons to accept moral nihilism, we should tentatively reject it. For we give up a lot by rejecting morality altogether. And if killing your mother for your inheritance doesn't differ morally from sending her flowers, then the moral enterprise falls apart. Fortunately, most of us don't believe we should kill our mothers. And we don't believe that our mothers should have killed us when we were young and helpless.

2. Determinism

Determinism is the view that every event has a cause. The doctrine claims that effects are the results of prior causes such that, given the cause, the effect will follow. Here is the deterministic argument in its simplest form:

- Actions are caused.
- Caused actions aren't free.
- Actions aren't free.

The entire universe seems governed by cause and effect. This universe obviously includes our brains, whose activity is caused by electrical signals, which in turn are caused by prior electrical activity, ad infinitum. The immediate causes of our behaviors are events in the brain, and we know that by stimulating the brain in various places we can make someone experience different things.

We can also make people act or move in certain ways by stimulating their brains, and they will experience the subsequent physical movements as natural. Moreover, when human brains are stimulated, people offer reasons why they subsequently moved their bodies. So it seems our decisions are determined too. And someone watching your brain scan sees the pattern that will result in your action, not only before you perform the action, but before you decide to perform the act. This is evidence that your decisions are determined.

Chapter 2 – Impediments to Ethical Theory

Not only do findings from the physical sciences count against our belief in free will, but so too does ordinary experience. Consider how much of what you do and believe can be predicted by the conditions of your upbringing, culture, socio-economic group, genome, gender, etc. This suggests that you didn't choose many of your behaviors and beliefs, but that they were forced upon you by your genes and environment.

Moreover, the science of psychology has little use for the concept of free will when explaining human actions. For example, behaviorism posits that humans are easily conditioned by positive and negative reinforcement; rules of classical and operant conditioning work are known to work with humans. Furthermore, experiments continually show that the conditions in which we find ourselves largely determine what we do. For example, in the famous Stanford prison experiment of the 1970s, we found that people can easily be turned into torturers. Furthermore, the experiments of Stanley Milgram found that many people will administer a near-fatal electric shock to another person because an authority asked them to.

So far we have placed the emphasis on the environment as the main factor that determines behavior. But there are also genes; there is also biology. Consider that psychologists have found that identical twins are remarkably similar even if raised in different environments. Identical twins reared together are the most alike; followed by twins reared apart, then siblings reared together, then siblings reared apart, then non-related kids reared together, then non-related kids reared apart. This is exactly what we should expect if genes and environment (plus random factors like genetic noise) determine behavior.

Moreover, we now know the connection between genes and: violence, alcoholism, impulsivity, OCD, depression, sexual orientation, and more. When you add genes and environment together it's hard to see how one is free. And even if we could resist the pull of biology and environment, the place for free will seems vanishingly small. The combination of genetic and environmental influences appears to be an exhaustive explanation of human behavior. The more science learns about people, the less likely it seems that they have free will.

But if determinism is true, then why ask: "what should we do?" If prior causes determine what we do, and these causes were themselves produced by other causes ad infinitum, then this chain of causality can be traced back to some state over which we had no control. We have no control over our genetic inheritance or the social environment into which we are born. So it makes no sense to say that we ought to do something, we are unable to do so. Ethicists often express this idea by saying that "ought implies can."

To understand the theory, ponder the following. You stand by an open window with a small child in your arms. Suddenly some maniac appears from behind you, pushes you and the child falls from your arms out the window to its untimely death. Certainly, you aren't responsible for the child's death. Now consider yourself by the window again, but this time the child is crying. Agitated, you suddenly throw the child out the window to its death. Now it seems you are responsible.

But wait. In *both* cases, something outside of you caused the child's death. In the first case the maniac was the cause, but what about the second case? Your agitated state was the cause of your throwing the child, but what caused that state? Perhaps you were stressed because you have a certain biochemistry that reacts violently to the stress caused by crying children, or perhaps you have no empathy because you were beaten as a child. So in both of our cases, we can trace a chain of causation backward to a situation over which we had no control. We had no control over why some people are psychopaths and knock babies from our arms, and we have no control over the myriad of physiological and environmental causes that led us to be the kind of people we are. None of us set our initial conditions. And if previous causes determine our choices, then it seems we are neither free nor responsible for our actions.

3. Responses to Determinism

There are multiple ways to respond to the determinist's challenge to free will and moral responsibility. The most common philosophical response is called *compatibilism*. It holds that freedom doesn't mean actions are uncaused, but that actions are uncoerced; freedom isn't actions without causes, but actions caused by individuals. So actions can be caused and still be free says the compatibilist.

To better understand this consider that uncaused actions would be random, but random actions aren't free actions. So free will *requires* that actions are caused! A person's character, desires, thoughts, and intentions cause behavior. And the fact that we can predict someone's behavior doesn't mean that they aren't free. Just because I know what you'll probably do doesn't mean that you didn't choose freely.

However, there are problems with compatibilism. For example, compatibilists say that we are free if our actions are uncoerced. But are actions ever uncoerced? It seems not, since character, desires, thoughts, intentions, preferences, desires, etc. are all caused by forces beyond our control. While there is much more to say about this issue, remember that *the majority of professional philosophers are compatibilists regarding free will*. And if they are correct, then determinism doesn't undermine free will or moral responsibility.

But even if we aren't free, we can still think of some actions or people as good or bad; so moral responsibility may survive even without free will. We can still say that torture is bad and medical care for children is good. Thus, even if we know why someone does the bad (good) things they do, the things they do are still bad (good). In that case, we might do best by setting up conditions that encourage moral behaviors. Hopefully, as we progress, we will adopt a therapeutic model to deal with immoral behavior, rather than our archaic retributionist model. In the end, free will may exist to some extent, but even if it doesn't the moral enterprise needn't collapse.

4. Psychological Egoism

Psychological egoism is a special kind of determinism. It says that self-interest motivates all human action even when it appears the interests of others sometimes motivates our actions. Consider a thief who murders his victims. He does so because he believes that was in his interest. Now consider someone who works with the poor. They also act because they think it's in their interest. They think such work will make them happy, better their soul, help them get to heaven, etc. According to psychological egoism, unselfish actions are impossible.

On the surface, this theory seems plausible. You want to join the Peace Corps because you think that is in your interest, while your friend wants to be a Wall Street banker because she thinks that's in her interest. Both of you do what you want to do, and psychological egoism is claiming that people *always* do what they want to do. That's how we are psychologically wired. The basic problem with this claim is that just because you do something doesn't mean you *wanted* to do it.

Chapter 2 – Impediments to Ethical Theory

In fact, people often do what they don't want to do. For instance, suppose I make an appointment to meet you tomorrow in my office, but in the meantime, a better opportunity arises. If I still keep my appointment with you, I am doing what I don't want to do. Now you might say that I kept the appointment because I'd feel guilty otherwise, or I thought I might lose my job by not performing my duties, but I could reply that I just wanted to do the right thing. Surely sometimes we do what we don't want to.

Another problem with the theory revolves around the distinction between self-interest and selfishness. If the theory maintains that we are always *selfish*—what we will call the strong version of psychological egoism—it's obviously false. Peace Corps volunteers aren't selfish since they act in other person's interests—the very definition of unselfishness. If the theory holds that we are always *self-interested*—the weak version of psychological egoism—then it fails too because we often act in non-self-interested ways. We smoke cigarettes; we overeat; we don't cultivate our minds. Thus, all actions aren't self-interested. We might object that people, though they don't always act in their self-interest, are motivated by self-interested. They smoke because they enjoy it, and fear the withdrawal effects if they quite. But this claim hardly stands up to scrutiny. The addicted smoker doesn't seem self-interested as much as they are self-destructive.

The theory does contain a trivial truth; people usually do what they want to. But the theory is mistaken when it reduces all human motivation to self-interest. Even if we are often motivated to act by our own interest, we may also be motivated by other people's interests. Sometimes we do things simply because we think we should do them. So even though self-interest is a powerful motivating force in human behavior, it isn't the only thing that motivates us. Psychological egoism is mistaken. People act from a variety of motives besides self-interest.

5. Ethical Egoism

While psychological egoism declares that we always *do* act in our own interest, ethical egoism claims that we *should* always act in our own interest. Psychological egoism *describes* the situation; ethical egoism *prescribes* what we should do. Ethical egoism is the doctrine which states that moral actions are self-interested actions, and individuals should be moral because it benefits them. This principle applies even if others will be hurt. If it's in my interest to steal your money and I can get away with it—then I should do it. However, ethical egoism also prescribes that I shouldn't try to steal your money if I can't get away with it—say because a police officer is nearby. If morality and self-interest coincide, then the egoist prescribes the moral act. If morality and self-interest conflict, then the egoist prescribes the immoral act. Egoists do whatever is in their self-interest.

There are many replies to the egoist. We might say they are immoral, will not go to heaven, will probably get caught, or will suffer from a guilty conscience. But they might not believe any of this. A better strategy against the egoist would be to point to the danger of a world made up exclusively of egoists. If we all act selfishly we will all be worse off. But the egoist may reply that they will prosper in this chaotic world by defeating their opponents. So they may choose to advocate morality, hide their egoism, and prosper against the naive. They might practice, but not advocate, their egoism.

In response, you might ask them: "how would you like it if others took advantage of you?" This is a complicated claim. Egoists agree they don't want *others* to be egoists because that wouldn't be in their interest. But why shouldn't *they* act egoistically? What do they care about another person's interests? How do others' interests give them a reason to do anything?

Chapter 2 – Impediments to Ethical Theory

Here we have entered into one of the most complex issues in contemporary philosophy. If others' interests give you a reason to act, then this refutes egoism. But if only your interests give you a reason to act, then egoism is irrefutable. Some distinguished contemporary philosophers—for example, the late Alan Gewirth of the University of Chicago, and Stephen Darwall, of Yale—argue for the former position while others—like Gilbert Harman of Princeton, and Kai Nielsen of the University of Calgary—argue for the latter. The problem of egoism has become particularly acute in the modern Western world since the rise of individualism in the eighteenth century. The emphasis on individual freedoms, rights, and privileges has lessened our concern for the community.

There is another problem with egoism which deserves investigation. It perplexes us that egoists should never publicly advocate their position. They don't want others to be egoists. But isn't this inconsistent? What does it mean to defend a theory which you can't publicly advocate? The contemporary philosopher Jesse Kalin defends egoism against the inconsistency charge. The egoist can consistently maintain, Kalin argues, that others ought to act in their own interest, but that doesn't mean the egoist wants them to. He gives the example of a chess game. I believe that you ought to move and put me in check, but that doesn't mean I want you to. Therefore, there isn't anything inconsistent about egoism.

Others reply that egoism blurs the distinction between the moral and non-moral uses of "ought," and it advocates a strange ethical system. Strange because the egoist must maintain that you really ought to knock them (the egoist) down and take their (the egoist's) wallet, but they (the egoist) sure hope you don't. Needless to say, this is a very unusual way of thinking about "ought," since ordinarily when we say someone ought to do something we want them to. Another contemporary philosopher, Brian Medlin, puts the point this way. Is it reasonable to say: "Of course you should do this, but for goodness sake don't?"

Medlin's attack on ethical egoism is controversial, and no argument probably convinces the egoist. When egoists ask why they shouldn't act immorally, perhaps our best reply is simply: "because someone might get hurt." If this response fails to convince them; no others will likely succeed.

6. Hedonism

Hedonism is the doctrine that the only intrinsic good is pleasure, and the only intrinsic evil is pain. The more pleasure and the less pain an action produces, the more intrinsically valuable it is. In its classic formulation, there are no differences drawn between the *qualities* of pleasure produced by an action; there are only differences in the *quantity* of pleasure. This means that for one person eating ice cream is more pleasurable than reading Shakespeare, while for others the reverse is true. According to the hedonist, you ought to choose that activity from the available choices which produces the greatest quantity of pleasure, or, if all the available choices are painful, you ought to choose the one with the least quantity of pain.

We might think of hedonism as a type of egoism. If egoism claims that you ought to do what is in your own self-interest, hedonism tells you what is ultimately in your interest—as much pleasure and as little pain as possible. This then raises the question of what life is most pleasurable. The initial response would seem to be a life filled with the sensual pleasures of food, drink, sex, psychological stimulation, etc. However, these activities are often accompanied by physical or psychological pain. How many people's lives are destroyed by their lack of temperance?

Chapter 2 – Impediments to Ethical Theory

Perhaps the most devastating critique of hedonism was offered by Plato in his dialogue the *Gorgias*. Gorgias agrees with Plato that it's pleasant to scratch an itch but, as Plato points out, if pleasure is the only good then a life spent itching and scratching would be a good life. So even if pleasure is good, surely it isn't the only good.

The ancient Greek philosopher Epicurus advanced a less radical version of hedonism. He advocated that we ought to seek mild pleasures that aren't accompanied by pain. So a moderate amount of food, drink, and sex is acceptable. (For example, we should develop refined tastes for a small glass of wine or the nuances of Eliot's poetry.) The problem is that such cultivated tastes take years to acquire, and entail sacrifice and hard work along the way. For all the virtues of such a doctrine, it barely resembles our initial version of hedonism.

This suggests that hedonism is either self-destructive or not specific enough to determine what we ought to do. Thus it's a beginning and not an end of our moral investigation. Let us now turn to perhaps the strongest impediment to ethical theorizing—moral relativism.

Chapter 3 – Cultural Moral Relativism

If anyone, no matter who, were given the opportunity of choosing from amongst all the nations in the world the set of beliefs which he thought best, he would inevitably—after careful considerations of their relative merits—choose that of his own country. Everyone without exception believes his own native customs, and the religion he was brought up in, to be the best. ~ Herodotus

1. What is Relativism?

Is LA close to New York City? Well, it's relative. LA is closer to NYC than it's to Mars, but it's not closer to NYC than it is to San Diego. Is rock-n-roll good music? Well, it depends. Most teenagers love it; many senior citizens don't. You may like rock, but your granddad likes Bach. In both cases, the answers depend upon what close or good is being measured against. Compared to Mars, LA and NYC are almost on top of each other; compared to San Diego, LA and NYC are a continent apart. Relative to my teenager's musical tastes, rock is better than Bach. As for me; I'd choose Bach over rock anytime. Now what about the logical law of non-contradiction, the distributive principle in arithmetic, the parallel postulate in Euclidean geometry, or atomic, evolutionary, and gravitation theories in science? Are these relative to, conditioned by, dependent upon, or measured against, something else? Or are they just true?

This kind of relativism we are talking about is called *epistemological relativism*. The idea is that there are no universal truths about the world, just different ways of interpreting it. The theory dates back at least to the ancient Greek philosopher Protagoras, but we can capture the basic idea with the following phrases:

Chapter 3 – Cultural Moral Relativism

- What you believe is true (for you); what I believe is true (for me).
- Truth is in the eye of the beholder.
- Different strokes for different folks.
- You have your beliefs; I have mine, and that's the end of it.

To be a relativist means that a belief, idea, proposition, claim, etc. is never true or false, good or bad, or right or wrong, *absolutely*. According to the relativist, there is no absolute or objective truth; truth is relative and subjective. For example, a relativist can't consistently claim that 2 + 2 = 4 because the answer 4 is neither right nor wrong. It just depends. Your math teacher likes 4, but you like 6; so for you, the answer is 6. And you can't consistently claim that gravity pulls objects downward, that airplanes fly because of aeronautical engineering principles, or that the earth is round since none of these are absolute truths—at least according to the relativist.

Consider some implications of relativism. If you are an art expert who loves Rembrandt, while your eight-year-old sister thinks her doodling is the best art, as a relativist you can't consistently maintain that your opinion about art is better than your sister's. And if you eat healthily, exercise, maintain an ideal weight, and engage in stress reduction activities; you can't consistently argue that your lifestyle is healthier than your roommate who eats poorly, lives a sedentary lifestyle, is overweight, and smokes to relieve stress. After all, it's all relative. Or suppose your brother has a Ph.D. in physics from Oxford and has recently found compelling evidence for superstring theory. As a relativist, you have no justification to say that your brother knows more about physical reality than your mother, who believes that she lives in a universe comprised of tiny, invisible gremlins whose gyrations are responsible for the expansion of the universe. After all, physicists have their view of reality and your Mom has hers, and that's the end of it.

2. Critique of Relativism

Do you really believe that the palm reader knows as much about the physical universe or the future as a physicist? (If you do, it's costing you money!) Do you believe that farmers know as much about medicine as physicians, or that auto mechanics know as much about the brain as neurophysiologists? Or that the principles of aeronautical engineering can fly planes, but holding hands and chanting "up, up, and away" works just as well? If you're a relativist you have to believe all these things, because nothing is true or false. But is everything just relative? You might say this, but do you really believe it? Would you rather drive over a bridge built by the army corps of engineers, or one made of duct tape built by psychics? Do you believe that the one bridge is as good as the other? Would you consult the next person you meet to determine if you need heart disease, or would you ask a cardiologist instead? And don't you ask experts because you assume there really are truths about the universe that the experts are more likely to know?

In addition to the outrageous implications of relativism, there are other reasons why relativism is problematic. Suppose I say "I think I'm a poached egg, the moon is made of cheese, and Elvis is alive and well in Mozambique, so these are true for me." What does this mean? To say that something is true—for you—doesn't add truth to a statement; it merely reports that you believe it. But here's the rub. Believing something doesn't make it true! You aren't a poached egg; the moon isn't made of cheese, and Elvis isn't alive and well in Mozambique. To respond that those statements are true for me is just silly because you're human, the moon is a rock, and

Chapter 3 – Cultural Moral Relativism

Elvis is dead. And those things are true for me, *and* for you! The truth is independent of your beliefs.

Moreover, relativism is logically incoherent. Consider the statement: all truth is relative. If this statement is objectively true, then relativism is false because there is at least one objective truth—namely, the truth that truth is relative. Thus, it's logically incoherent to say, all truth is relative is objectively true. But if the statement is only subjectively true, then this just means that you believe in relativism. So by claiming that truth is relative you either contradict yourself or make a trivial claim with nothing to recommend your belief. It seems relativism is either objectively false, in which case you shouldn't be a relativist; or relativism is subjectively false, in which case you don't believe in it.

In response, a relativist could claim that the proposition that the truth is relative is the one objectively true proposition, while all other propositions are relative. So the only true proposition is: all truth is relative except the claim that truth is relative. Apart from wondering why such a puzzling proposition is true, we also wonder if this modified proposition is objectively or subjectively true. If objectively true, then you have again contradicted yourself, inasmuch as you have to admit that this new proposition is absolute; if subjectively true, then again you have merely made the trivial claim that you believe in relativism. And of course, if this new proposition is objectively or subjectively false, you haven't helped your case at all.

In reply, you could construct a new proposition: all truth is relative except the claim that "all truth is relative except the claim that all truth is relative." (Hang on if you feel you need a beer!) This is known as an infinite regress argument; you continue to construct a new claim to infinity. But whatever proposition you advance, we can always show that what you're claiming is either a contradiction or just states your belief in relativism. Now you don't want to be contradicting yourself because that's just silly. And you don't want to say that you believe in relativism because you just believe in it. Thus relativism is either self-refuting or trivial.

3. Relativism, the Unknown, and Belief

Relativism also seduces because you might confuse your inability to know the truth with there being no truth. I don't know if intelligent life exists elsewhere in the universe, but intelligent life either does or doesn't exist elsewhere—my inability to determine the truth is irrelevant to the actual truth about the matter. You may not know whether a God exists or not, or if the author of this text is married with children, but God either exists or doe not, and I either do or don't have a wife and children. The fact that you don't know what 2 + 2 equals doesn't mean there is no solution to the problem; it means your bad at arithmetic. Therefore, your inability to distinguish between truth and falsity isn't evidence for the truth of relativism.

This leads to a related idea. Don't confuse the fervency of your belief with a belief being true. You may be convinced the universe is teeming with intelligent life, that a God exists, or that the author of this text has six wives, but this doesn't mean these beliefs are true. Remember that you often believe things that are mistaken. You may believe that continental drift is impossible, that biological evolution didn't happen, or that relativity theory is bogus. But your belief hasn't anything to with the truth or falsity of these ideas. Therefore, the strength of your belief in something—say that all truth is relative—isn't evidence for the truth of relativism.

4. Summary of Relativism

Ok, let's see where we've been so far. The claim that all truth is relative is either incoherent or trivial. Moreover, relativism is

Chapter 3 – Cultural Moral Relativism

neither supported by our inability to know what's true, nor by the fervency of our belief in relativism. But does this mean that nothing is relative? No. The answers to all the following questions are relative. Is LA close to NYC? Does chocolate taste better than vanilla? Who's the world's greatest athlete? Is Messerly a great philosopher? It's not the claim that some things are relative that has been positively refuted; rather, it's the claim that all things are relative that is incoherent or illogical. And if all things aren't relative and subjective, then some things must be absolute and objective.

Now you might agree that this assault on relativism has been successful, but still claim that while some truths are objective—logical, mathematical, and natural scientific ones for example—other so-called truths are relative—say ethical truths. Such considerations lead us to *moral relativism*, the theory that there is no absolute, objective, and universally binding moral truths. According to the moral relativist, there exist conflicting moral claims that are both true. (X can be both right and wrong at the same time.) In short, ethical relativists deny that there is any objective truth about right and wrong. Ethical judgments aren't true or false because there is no objective moral truth for a moral judgment to correspond to. In brief, morality is relative, subjective, and non-universally binding and disagreements about ethics are like disagreements about what flavor of ice cream is best.

What then is morality relative to? To a group's or individual's beliefs, emotions, opinions, wants, desires, interests, preferences, feelings, etc. We now distinguish between two kinds of moral relativism: cultural moral relativism and personal moral relativism.

5. What is Cultural Moral Relativism?

Cultural moral relativism is the theory that moral judgments or truths are relative to cultures. Consequently, what is right in one society may be wrong in another and vice versa. (For culture, you may substitute: nation; society; group, sub-culture; etc.) This is another theory with ancient roots. Herodotus, the father of history, describes the Greeks encounter with the Callatians who ate their dead relatives. Naturally, the Greeks found this practice revolting. But the Callatians were equally repelled by the Greek practice of cremation causing Herodotus to conclude that ethics is culturally relative. In fact, different cultures do have different moral codes. The Incas practiced human sacrifice, Eskimos shared their wives with strangers and killed newborns in certain situations, Japanese samurais tried out their new swords on innocent passers-by, Europeans enslaved Africans, and female circumcision is performed today in parts of Africa.

Cultural moral relativism contains two theses: 1) the *diversity* thesis—moral beliefs, practices, and values are diverse or vary from one culture to another; and 2) the *dependency* thesis—moral obligations depends upon cultures since cultures are the final arbiters of moral truth. In short, cultural relativism implies that no cultural values have any objective, universal validity, and it would be arrogant for one culture to make moral judgments about other cultures.

The thesis of *diversity is descriptive*; it describes the way things are. Moral beliefs, rules, and practices, in fact, depend upon facets of culture like social, political, religious, and economic institutions. By contrast, the thesis of *dependency is prescriptive*; it describes how things ought to be. Morality should depend on culture because there isn't anything else upon which it's based. Now we might argue for cultural relativism as follows:

Chapter 3 – Cultural Moral Relativism

Argument 1 – (from the diversity thesis)

- Different cultures have different moral codes;
- Thus, there is no morality independent of culture.

The weakness of this argument is that the conclusion doesn't follow from the premise. The fact that cultures disagree about morality doesn't show that morality is relative. After all, cultures disagree about whether abortion is moral or immoral, but their disagreement doesn't mean there is no truth about the matter. It might be that one culture is just mistaken. Consider how cultures might disagree as to whether the earth or sun is at the center of our solar system. Their disagreement doesn't mean there is no truth about the matter. Similarly, societies might disagree about whether they should put their young to death, but that disagreement proves nothing, other than societies disagree. Thus cultural disagreements, by themselves, aren't enough to prove cultural relativism. Now consider another argument for cultural relativism:

Argument 2 – (from the dependency thesis)

- Moral truths depends on cultural beliefs;
- Thus, there is no moral truth independent of culture.

The argument commits the fallacy that logicians call "begging the question." This occurs when you assume the truth of what you are trying to prove. (For example, if you ask me why I think abortion is wrong and I say, because it's bad, I've begged the question.) In argument 2, one is trying to show that right and wrong depend on culture, but it begs the question to say that right and wrong depend on culture because they depend on culture.

6. Critique of Cultural Moral Relativism – Part 1

Now suppose we put the two theses together? That will give us the strongest argument for cultural relativism.

Argument 3 – (from both the diversity and dependency thesis)

- Right and wrong vary between cultures (diversity).
- Right and wrong depend upon cultures (dependency).
- Thus, right and wrong are relative to culture.

This seems better; at least the conclusion follows from the premises. But are these premises true? Let's consider the first premise (diversity). Nothing seems more obvious than the fact of cultural differences. Eskimos believed in infanticide; most Americans don't. Many Americans believe that solitary confinement is a just punishment; most French find the practice barbaric. Clearly, there are different cultural mores. But maybe the differences between cultural values *aren't as great as they seem*.

Consider that Eskimos live in harsh climates where food is in short supply and mothers nurse their babies for years. There simply isn't enough food for all their children, nor enough backs upon which nomadic people can carry their children. So Eskimos want their children to live just like we do, and it's the harsh and unusual condition that force them to make difficult choices. Sometimes they kill a weaker child so that both the stronger and weaker children won't die. We may disagree with the practice, but we can imagine doing the same in similar circumstances. Thus, the underlying principle—life is valuable—has been applied differently in different contexts. So maybe cultures aren't so different after all.

Now consider that there is more crime in America than in France. Most Americans seem to believe that criminals deserve to be

Chapter 3 – Cultural Moral Relativism

punished for their crimes, that severe punishment brings peace to the victim's family, that capital punishment is a deterrent to crime, etc. The French are more likely to renounce retribution or doubt that capital punishment brings victim's families peace or deters crime. But notice again. Both cultures are steered by a principle—act justly—even though they apply the principle differently. So upon closer inspection, there doesn't seem to be as much disagreement as it first appeared. So the differences in cultural values might be more apparent than real.

Now suppose we also could show that there are moral principles that all cultures share? Wouldn't that show that morality wasn't relative to culture? Many scientists claim that there are moral principles common to all cultures. For instance, all cultures share: regulations on sexual behavior; prohibitions against unjust killing; requirements of familial obligations and child care; emphasis on truth-telling; and reward for reciprocity and cooperation. If we take these two ideas together—cultural moral differences aren't as great as they appear, and all cultures do share some moral values—then the *diversity thesis is false*. And if the first premise is false, then the conclusion of the cultural relativist's argument doesn't follow.

However, notice that even if the first premise is false, that doesn't prove that moral objectivism is true. Cultures that share the same moral values could all be wrong. So the empirical evidence concerning similarities and differences between moral codes isn't relevant to the question of whether morality is absolute or relative. And that means that while we haven't proven the truth of cultural absolutism, we have undermined the cultural relativist. For if the evidence about the diversity of culture is irrelevant, then we have undermined the relativist's first premise, and with it the conclusion of his/her argument.

7. Critique of Cultural Moral Relativism – Part 2

While undermining the first premise sufficiently undermines cultural relativism, let's turn to the second premise (dependency) to see if it fares any better. Now it does appear true that some moral "truths" depend on culture—for example, regulations on sexual behaviors or funeral practices. But it isn't self-evident that *all* moral truth depends on culture. Moral truth may be independent of culture in the same way that other truths are independent of culture. Ethics may be objectively grounded in reason, the god's commands, the most happiness for the most people, human nature, or something else.

But rather than trying to contradict all the relativist's arguments for the second premise, consider the implications of taking cultural relativism seriously. If cultural relativism is true then all of the following (counter-intuitive) are true. 1) We can't make cross-cultural judgments. We can't consistently criticize a culture for killing all those over forty, exterminating ethnic groups, or banishing children to the Antarctic. 2) We can't make intra-cultural judgments. We can't say, even within our culture, whether we should send children to their death or to school, whether we should torture our criminals or rehabilitate them. 3) The idea of moral progress is incoherent. All you can say is that cultures change, not that one is better than another. The old culture practiced slavery; we don't, and that's the end of it. The appearance of moral progress is illusory.

But all this is strongly counter-intuitive. We might think that cultures can do what they want regarding funeral practices, but what about human sacrifice? Aren't there some things that are just wrong in all cultures? Don't you believe that society is better now because it has outlawed slavery? And if cultural relativism says

Chapter 3 – Cultural Moral Relativism

that anything is permissible, can such a counterintuitive theory be correct?

It seems then that cultural relativism is as incoherent and unsubstantiated as epistemological relativism. The logical arguments for cultural relativism fail, and we have good reasons to doubt the truth of the premises of cultural relativism. Finally, cultural relativism contradicts our moral intuition. While we may not have proven the theory mistaken, we have shown that there are many reasons to doubt the theory, and few reasons to accept it.

Chapter 4 – Personal Moral Relativism

[Human are] the measure of all things. ~ Protagoras

1. What is Personal Moral Relativism?

If morality isn't relative to culture, might it be relative to a person's beliefs, attitudes, emotions, opinions, desires, wants, etc.? *Personal relativism* is a theory that holds that moral judgments are relative to, conditioned by, or dependent upon, individuals. This theory has ancient roots but is also popular today. These remarks capture the basic idea:

- You have your opinion, and I have mine.
- Truth is relative to my beliefs.
- My belief is true for me, while yours is true for you.
- You do your thing, and I'll do mine.

Analogous to the cultural relativist, the personal relativist claims that there is no objective moral truth. For instance, relativists say that while some hate homosexuality and others don't, there is no objective truth about whether homosexuality is right or wrong. Instead moral statements merely report opinions, feelings, and attitudes; they just tell you what people prefer. To say that x is right/good/moral, just means you like, favor, or approve of x. To say that x is wrong/bad/immoral, simply means that you dislike, disfavor, or disapprove of x. In other words, moral truth is relative; it's subjective. (Personal moral relativism is also called ethical subjectivism.)

But notice that, according to personal relativism, there is a way that a moral judgment can be true or false. If we say homosexuality is moral and we're telling the truth, then it's true that we think

Chapter 4 – Personal Moral Relativism

homosexuality is moral. If we're lying, then it's false that we think homosexuality is moral. Of course, moral judgments aren't objectively true or false according to personal relativism since there is no standard independent of a person's feelings, but they are subjectively true or false, if we report our beliefs truthfully.

2. Critique of Personal Relativism

Personal relativism is open to the same objections as was epistemological and cultural relativism, as the following questions suggest. What does it mean to say something is true for me? Is the claim that truth is relative to me, relatively or absolutely true? If the former, relativism is inconsistent, if the latter, relativism is trivial. Is there as much individual moral disagreement as it appears, or is most moral disagreements on the surface only? Don't most people share common moral beliefs? Don't the consequences of taking this theory seriously conflict with our moral intuition? Aren't some actions just plain wrong?

Given our previous critique, we should reject personal relativism at first glance. Why then is the theory so appealing? Maybe personal relativism attracts us because it reminds us that not everything we believe is true. Perhaps it helps us be open to new ideas. Or maybe we accept it because others do. Whatever the reason we find relativism compelling, let's consider it in detail.

Consider the following. If I enjoy torturing small children in the most painful way possible, do you think that's ok? Do you believe that whether this is right or wrong depends on me? Or do you think it's just plain wrong? Remember, if personal relativism is true then there isn't anything wrong with torturing small children. But you don't believe that. And you don't believe that Gandhi and Hitler were moral equivalents because you think that good and bad are in some sense objective. That's why you think there is something wrong with torturing children, and any moral theory that suggests otherwise must be flawed.

To believe that torturing children is morally acceptable is counter-intuitive. As we have seen it's true that our intuition isn't always a good guide. But if a moral theory leads to consequences that contradict a strongly held moral intuition, then we are justified in questioning that moral theory. If a moral theory advocates torture, and nearly everyone thinks torture is immoral, we should probably reject such a theory unless there are other compelling reasons not to. So the claim that a theory is strongly counter-intuitive doesn't prove that it's wrong, but it counts as a reason to reject that theory.

Consider another intuitive argument against moral relativism. Suppose I gave you an F on your ethics test, even though I admit that your answers were perfect. Puzzled, you ask why you received an F, and I tell you that I don't like you. Furthermore, I tell you that your friend received an A because I really like her. What would you think about this? Wouldn't you feel that this was unfair? If so, you're assuming there is some objective standard of fairness independent of the professor. However, if you're a relativist, consistency demands that you accept that your grade is relative to whether I like you or not. But you think your grade on the test shouldn't be relative to the professor because that's not fair. So you do think that there is an objective standard of fairness.

There is something else peculiar about personal relativism. It's easy to say that you are a relativist, but it's hard to actually be a relativist. If the beliefs of child-torturers and child-lovers conflict, the relativist says that they're both correct. And while you can say this, it's hard to believe it. In fact, when confronted with moral disagreements, we make judgments and debate what we should believe and do. In practice, we act as if what we do matters as if some courses of action and some beliefs are morally preferable to others. In practice, it's virtually impossible to be a relativist. We do think that it is wrong for samurai swordsmen to try out his new sword on an innocent passer-by.

3. Tolerance and Relativism

Tolerance is generally a good thing. I don't want my neighbors to exterminate me because I philosophize too much; I'm sure they don't want me to attack them because they watch too much TV. Tolerance is good, serving to remind us that we may be mistaken about our beliefs or the moral appropriateness of our actions. But what is the relationship between moral relativism and tolerance? Does accepting the theory of moral relativism lead to tolerance?

In the first place, there is a contradiction between tolerance and moral relativism. If you're a relativist, then you can't consistently defend tolerance as a universal value. If you do, then you're not a relativist, you're an absolutist for whom tolerance is an objective value. So relativism and tolerance are logically incompatible.

Now suppose I am a moral relativist. As a relativist, I may be tolerant of your views, but I may also decide that I can do anything I want to you—say, torture and kill you because there isn't anything wrong with that. After all, it's just relative. As a relativist, I might be tolerant of you, but I might not. So there doesn't seem to be a necessary connection between relativism and tolerance.

Now suppose I am a moral absolutist. As an absolutist, I may be intolerant of your views, but I may also be tolerant of them. So it's hard to see any connection between moral objectivism or relativism and tolerance. Moral relativism may lead to tolerance or intolerance, as may moral absolutism. In the end, neither moral relativism nor moral objectivism relates directly to tolerance.

In the end, we just don't know what the relationship between moral theory and practice is, which is probably obvious from your experience. Ethics professors may espouse moral theories, but they may be horrific people. The religious may espouse charity but steal the Sunday collection. Theories about how we should act, often don't translate into action. So even if there should be a connection between moral relativism and tolerance, it doesn't seem there is one.

On closer examination tolerance doesn't appear affected by the content of your belief; rather, tolerance is affected by how certain you are of what you believe. If you're certain that you know the truth about something, then you will likely be intolerant; if you're less certain you know the truth about something, you will likely be more tolerant. If we value tolerance then, we should be humble.

4. Emotivism

The English philosopher A.J. Ayer (1910 – 1989) and the American philosopher Charles Stevenson (1908 – 1979) developed a more extreme version of personal relativism. Emotivism is a theory that claims that moral language or judgments: 1) are neither true nor false; 2) express our emotions; and 3) try to influence others to agree with us. To better understand emotivism, consider the following statements:

- The Earth is larger than Jupiter.
- The St. Louis Cardinals won the World Series in 1964.

You may not know whether these claims are true or false, but both are declarative statements that are *either* true or false; they have cognitive content. Now consider the following:

- Go Manchester United!
- That's bull!

Chapter 4 – Personal Moral Relativism

Both are exclamatory statements that are *neither* true nor false; they have no cognitive content. They express emotions and try to influence others to share the emotion.

Emotivists believe that moral language expresses emotions and tries to influence others. If I say homosexuality is evil, I'm just expressing my feeling that homosexuality is disgusting! I am expressing my emotions and, at the same time, trying to influence you to dislike homosexuality. The same analysis applies to any moral judgment. If I say that abortion is wrong, I'm just expressing my dislike for it and trying to get you to agree with me. I might as well have said "abortion," while shaking my head and rolling my eyes. And if I say that Joseph Stalin or Dick Cheney were bad men, I'm merely trying to get you to agree with what I'm saying.

Now the difference between emotivism and personal relativism (subjectivism) is subtle. When personal relativists say Gandhi was a good man they are reporting their view of Gandhi. And this report is true or false depending on whether they are telling the truth. But the emotivist claims there is no truth or falsity to moral judgments whatsoever. If I say I hate abortion—assuming I'm being sincere—then this expressed emotion is neither true nor false, it just is. In other words, the emotivist says that different moral judgments are just like differences in taste. I like carrots; you don't. I like homosexuality; you don't. But emotivists don't consider moral judgments as *reporting* attitudes; instead moral judgments *express* attitudes. In the same way that cows moo, humans emote. Therefore, according to the emotivists, moral language has no factual content at all, and it can't be true or false in any way.

Now, why would one think that moral language is just disguised emotional expression? Ayer thought that moral language was meaningless because it couldn't be verified. If I say that there's a dollar on my desk, you know what I mean and you can verify or falsify my statement—you just go look. But if I say that lying is bad, how you could verify this? Where would you go to see that lying was bad? Ayer argued that statements that couldn't be verified were meaningless. There is no meaning to propositions like abortion is immoral because there is no way to show such statements are true or false.

While Stevenson granted that moral language didn't have factual or cognitive content, he argued that it had emotive meaning. Moral propositions aren't true or false, but they aren't meaningless either—moral language expresses emotions. Thus he could easily account for our differences regarding ethics—we have different emotions. And when we disagree, Stevenson said we have a *disagreement in attitude*.

5. Critique of Emotivism

Do moral judgments function exclusively to express emotions? If I say that Gandhi was a good man, I'm expressing my emotions, trying to influence you, and I'm making a moral judgment. On the other hand, aren't I doing more? Don't I believe that Gandhi was good in comparison with some standard of goodness? After all, I'm not just saying Gandhi, and then smiling. So when I say Gandhi was good I express my fond feelings for him, and I want you to feel the same, but that doesn't mean that's all I'm doing. I almost certainly believe that Gandhi was good in a way that Dick Cheney wasn't. So while a moral judgment isn't exactly the same as a factual judgment, it isn't exactly the same as exclamatory judgments either. Why?

Consider how I would go about persuading you that Gandhi was good, while Cheney wasn't. I might appeal to his selflessness working with the poor, his devotion to his friends and country, the

Chapter 4 – Personal Moral Relativism

positive effect he had on strangers, or his ritual of daily meditation. And by doing this I'm giving you reasons for thinking he was a good person. I also point out that Cheney masterminded the extermination and torture of thousands, had a violent temper, was unpleasant company, was in the Nixon administration, has no remorse for anything he ever did, and never meditated. Again my opponents might not be persuaded. Maybe killing and torturing thousands is a good thing, and being peaceful is an awful thing.

But notice that you're asking me for reasons, and I am giving you plenty of reasons why Gandhi was a better person than Cheney—reasons that most rational persons would accept assuming my claims are true. And whenever I give reasons, I'm doing more than just expressing emotions; I'm assuming that there is more to moral claims than emotions. If not, why try to convince someone? True, I could try to convince someone by merely continuing to express my emotions. But my emoting wouldn't convince a rational person. So it seems that objective reason must play some role in ethics.

Certainly, it's true that some people might not be convinced by good reasons, but that doesn't mean that I didn't give them good reasons, or that reasons are unimportant. It might just be that they won't accept the good reasons I have given them. Thus, if you point out that my disliking you is irrelevant to what you deserve on a test, then you have given me a good reason why you shouldn't have failed. And we can probably think of many examples when we give others good reasons to do or believe something and they just won't listen. This appealing to reasons to persuade suggests that we use moral language to do more than just express emotions.

Therefore, emotivism presupposes that moral disagreements are incapable of being resolved by rational discourse. There is no way to resolve our attitudinal disagreements unless we are persuasive or violent enough. But we have already seen that there's another way to persuade—using reason to support our position. We can provide good reasons why x is right or x is wrong. If we appeal to reason, then we have discovered how to resolve our disputes with others without shouting or beating them into submission. And if reason plays a role in ethics, then there is truth or falsity about ethical judgments. Thus emotivism must not be the whole story.

6. Conclusion

Some things aren't relative—throw this book out the classroom window and it will fall. Some elements of morality may be relative, but surely not all of them—you shouldn't kill your good friend because he owes you a dollar. Tolerance is a generally a good thing, but there is no special connection between it and relativism. We do express ourselves and try to influence others when we make moral judgments, but that's only a small part of what we do. Killing an innocent person could possibly be justified, but are you ever justified in torturing someone for your own pleasure or amusement? As long as you answer no to this question, you aren't a relativist. But even if ethics is objective, why should I abide by its dictates? Why shouldn't I just seek pleasure? Why shouldn't I just do whatever I want? To answer these questions, we turn to moral theories.

Chapter 5 – Natural Law Theory

To disparage the dictates of reason is equivalent to condemning the command of God. ~ Thomas Aquinas

1. The Divine Command Theory

Let us now consider the view that morality rests upon religion. Assuming that a relationship between a god and morality exists, how do we characterize it? One classic formulation of this relationship is called *the divine-command theory*. (DCT) According to DCT, things are right or wrong simply because the gods command or forbid them. There is nothing more to morality. It's like a parent who says to a child: it's right because I said so.

To answer the question of whether morality can be based on a god we would have to know: 1) if there are gods; 2) if the gods are good; 3) if the gods issue commands; 4) if the commands are good ones; 5) how to find the commands; 6) how to understand or interpret the commands; 7) the proper version and translation of holy books issuing commands, the proper interpretation of some revelation of the commands, or the legitimacy of a church authority issuing commands, etc.

Consider just the interpretation problem. When, for example, does a command like, "thou shalt not kill" apply? In self-defense? In war? Always? And to whom does it apply? To animals? Intelligent aliens? Serial killers? All living things? The unborn? The brain dead? Religious commands such as "don't kill," "honor thy parents," or "don't commit adultery" are ambiguous. Difficulties also arise if we hear voices commanding us, or we accept an institutions' authority. Why trust the voices in our heads or authorities or institutions? Obviously, there are enormous philosophical difficulties with basing ethics on religion.

But let's say for the sake of argument that there are gods, that you have found the right one, that the right one issued commands, that the commands are good, that you have access to the right commands (because you found the right book, church, or had the right vision or heard the right voices), that you understand the commands, and that you interpret the commands correctly even though they came from a book that has been translated from one language to another over a period of thousands of years. (Anyone who has ever translated knows that you can't translate word for word between languages.) Let's just say that somehow you are right about everything. Can you then base ethics on religion?

2. Plato's Question

More than 2,000 years ago, in Plato's dialogue *Euthyphro*, Socrates asked a famous question which roughly translates: "Are things right because the gods command them, or do the gods command them because they are right?" If things are right simply because the gods command them, then their commands are arbitrary—there are no good reasons for their commands. The gods then are like petty tyrants who just command things because they have the power. In addition, another problem is that DCT reduces the notion of a god's goodness to nonsense. To say that x is good simply means that x is commanded by God. So DCT is flawed.

On the other hand, if the gods command things *because* they are right, then there are reasons for their commands. The gods command things because they see or recognize that certain commands are really good for us. But if that is the case, then there is some standard, norm or criteria by which good or bad are measured. And this standard is independent of the gods.

So either the god's command are without reason, and therefore arbitrary, or they are with reason, and thus are commanded

Chapter 5 – Natural Law Theory

according to some standard. This standard—say that we would all be better off—is thus the reason we should be moral. And that reason, not a god's authority—is what makes something right or wrong. And the same is true for an authoritative book. Something isn't wrong simply because the book says so. There must be a reason that something is right or wrong and if there isn't, then the book has no authority.

Of course one could argue that even if the gods are petty tyrants who command us without reason—except say for their own amusement—we should still follow the commands so as not to suffer—since the gods are powerful and vindictive enough to do so. If they can inflict eternal torture—if they are sadists—then we do have a reason to follow their commands—to avoid torture!

The response to this is that we don't know that the gods will reward us for following their arbitrary commands. Maybe the gods reward people who use their reason and don't accept such commands and punish those who are so frightened as to accept non-rational commands. This seems to make some sense if the gods are petty, tyrannical bullies, they might like it if you stood up to them. Who knows?

The foregoing discussion should suffice to show how difficult it is to base ethics on religion. Again, even if one could overcome all the practical difficulties involved in philosophically justifying religion, it seems that either: a) the god's commands are arbitrary, and there is thus no reason to follow those commands; or b) the god's commands aren't arbitrary, and there are reasons for the commands. But if the latter is the case, then we are doing philosophical, not theological, ethics. We are looking for the reasons why things are moral or immoral and the gods become irrelevant to that pursuit.

Finally, you might object that the gods have reasons for their commands, and we just can't know them. But if this is the case, if we can't know anything about the gods' reasons, if the ways of the gods "are mysterious to humans," then what's the point of religion? If you can't know anything why the gods command things, then why follow their commands, why have religion at all, why listen to the priest or preacher? If it's all a mystery, then no person or book or church has anything coherent to say about God, ethics, or anything else.

If we want to rationally justify morality, then we will have to advance a moral theory independent of hypothetical gods. We will have to engage in philosophical ethics.

3. The History of Natural Law Ethics

The genesis of *natural law ethics* is in the writings of Aristotle, who first identified the natural with the good. All things "aim at some good," he says at the beginning of his treatise on ethics, "and for this reason, the good has rightly been declared that at which all things aim." For individuals, ethics is a study of the goal, end or purpose of human life. Politics, on the other hand, is a study of the good, goal, end, or purpose of society.

But what is good? Aristotle distinguished between real and apparent goods. *Real goods* satisfy natural needs, and they are good for us independent of our desires. Food, clothing, and shelter are examples of real goods. *Apparent goods* satisfy acquired wants and are called good because we desire them. Shrimp, designer clothes, and mansions are apparent goods. A good life consists in the acquisition, over the course a lifetime, of all the real (natural) goods. These include external and bodily goods such as food, clothing, shelter, health, vitality, and vigor, and, "goods of the soul" like love, friendship, knowledge, courage, justice, honor, and skill. To obtain these real goods requires that we must act with good habits or virtues. The person of good character exhibits moral virtues such as temperance, courage, and justice, and intellectual virtues like wisdom and prudence. A life full of virtue is a good, happy, and fulfilling life. It is a life in accordance with our nature.

The idea that each thing has a goal or purpose in accordance with its nature, Aristotle called *teleology*. (From the Greek telos; meaning goal, end, or purpose.) We can understand this if we consider an artifact like a pen. A pen that writes well is a good pen; it fulfills its purpose. Aristotle also believed that teleology was also a component of the natural world. Acorns develop into oak trees, caterpillars into butterflies, and little children into mature adults; the eyes are meant to see, the hands to grasp, and the kidneys to purify. Whatever satisfies its teleology is fulfilled; whatever fails to do so is defective. To be fulfilled means to actualize the potential inherent in the thing, whereas to be defective refers to the failure to do so. And things that fulfill their teleology are good. The actualization of natural potential is the essence of teleology and supplies the moral imperative for human beings.

The Stoics further developed the doctrine and first used the term natural law. Stoicism flourished in Athens in the third century B.C.E. and later in the Roman Empire in such great figures as Seneca, Epictetus, Marcus Aurelius, and Cicero. Unlike Aristotle, the Stoics believed that human happiness was possible without external and bodily goods. They also emphasized rationality and the control of emotions. The Stoics insisted that we have a duty to follow nature, particularly our rational nature, rather than convention. The source of natural law was Logos, the universal power or energy personified in nature's laws.

That natural law should prevail over cultural conventions led the Stoics to the idea of the cosmopolitan citizen. Roman jurisprudence, which needed to formulate rules to deal with various cultures, adopted the idea of a natural law for all the world's citizens. Its basic premise was the natural law's independence from cultural mores.

This idea had tremendous repercussions throughout human history, and it would inform the interaction of Western Europe and much of the new world. In the sixteenth century, for instance, the Spaniards vehemently debated its applicability for the civilizations they discovered in the New World, and in the eighteenth century, the idea influenced the founders of the American government. But the next great development in the idea of the natural law after the Stoics occurred in the thirteenth century.

4. St. Thomas Aquinas

St. Thomas Aquinas (1225– 1274) synthesized Aristotelianism, Stoicism, and Christianity to give the natural law its classic formulation. In addition to Aristotle's natural virtues, he added the theological virtues faith, hope, and charity. And to earthly happiness, he added eternal beatitude. For Thomas, action in accordance with human nature fulfills God's eternal plan and Scripture's commandments. Thus the natural law is God's law known to human reason. Unlike the lower animals, we have the ability to understand the laws of our nature, and the free will to follow or disregard these laws.

But how do we attain knowledge of the natural law? It isn't innate, intuited, or easily derived from sense experience. Instead, we use reason to determine the conformity of moral conduct and nature. Since fulfilling natural needs makes us happy, the natural is the good. What then constitutes the law? While all mature

Chapter 5 – Natural Law Theory

individuals know its most general principles like don't kill the innocent, controversy surrounds reasoned conclusions about its specific applications.

The fundamental principle of natural law ethics is that good should be done and evil avoided. This general principle may be specified into moral axioms like: "Don't kill!" "Be faithful!" "Preserve your life!" "Care for your children!" "Don't lie or steal!" "Life is a universal human good!" All of these axioms are both natural and good. We further specify these axioms by rational analysis and by reliance on Church, scripture, or revelation. As Aristotle pointed out, natural inclinations and tendencies are good, and we fulfill them by acquiring the elements which constitute human happiness such as: life, procreation, friendship, and knowledge. Nevertheless, within the boundaries set by human nature, the specific way one satisfies natural inclinations may differ. So a range of activities might satisfy, for instance, our aesthetic or intellectual needs. However, we all need the universal human goods. Thus, morality demands that we follow the laws of our nature which are the same for all on the basis of our shared humanity.

Still, we need not satisfy all of our natural tendencies. For instance, we must curb aggression and dishonesty, so that friendship and society thrive. In this way, we see how reason makes value judgments and imposes moral obligations upon us. The moral law demands that we develop our reason, and act in accordance with reason's imperatives. As we have seen, nature directs us to live well, flourish in human communities, and, finally, to experience the beatific vision of God. Therefore, beginning with human nature and using reason to determine the goals nature sets for us, we determine what we ought to do.

Perhaps a simple illustration may help. If we want to become nurses, then we ought to go to college and study nursing. Employing our rational faculties, we impose a non-moral obligation upon ourselves, given an antecedent goal or purpose. Analogously, reason imposes moral obligations upon us. If we want friends and friendship demands justice, then we ought to be just. Of course, the examples are very different. Moral obligations may not depend upon self-interest in the same way that non-moral obligations do. But the basic idea is the same, without goals nothing is obligatory. If we don't want to be nurses or don't want friends, then we probably have no obligation to study nursing or be just. And if there are no ultimate purposes in human life, then there probably are no moral obligations either. On the other hand, according to the natural law, the complete actualization of human potential demands that we are just and develop our talents. If we fail to do this, we violate the natural law.

5. Some Philosophical Difficulties

Natural law theory derives values about what we ought to do from facts about our human nature. This is a major philosophical difficulty. When we derive what we ought to do from what is the case, we commit what philosophers call the *naturalistic fallacy*. This fallacy involves the derivation of ethical conclusions from non-ethical facts. But isn't there a logical gap between what is the case and what ought to be the case? Even if it's true, for instance, that humans are naturally aggressive, does that mean they should be? Though a conception of human nature is relevant to morality, it seems unlikely that one could explain morality by appealing to human nature. (Yet, if values don't come from facts, where do they come from?)

A second difficulty with the theory is that modern science rejects teleology. Explanations in science don't refer to goals, values, or

Chapter 5 – Natural Law Theory

purposes. Rocks don't fall because they desire to get to the earth's center, as Aristotle thought, nor does it rain in order to make plants grow. Rather, physical reality operates according to impersonal laws of cause and effect. Evolutionary theory rejects teleology and all of cosmic evolution results from a series of fortuitous occurrences. This brings to light another difficulty. Natural law theory traditionally maintains the immutability of human nature, which contradicts modern biology. Furthermore, technology transforms human nature. What happens when gene splicing, recombinant DNA, and genetic engineering become normal? For various reasons then, natural law as traditionally conceived and modern science are at odds.

6. Final thoughts

Of course, the fact that, with the exception of the Catholic Church, the theory of natural law has fallen into disfavor doesn't mean that it's mistaken. If we believe that we can demonstrate the existence of a source of values and purposes for human beings, and believe also that knowledge of this source is accessible to human reason, then we may rationally defend the theory. Furthermore, without such presuppositions, moral thinking is likely futile. A number of contemporary philosophers suggest that without some ultimate, objective source for morality, notions like obligation, duty, right, and good make no sense.

Nevertheless, natural law theory does rest upon a number of dubious philosophical propositions. We shouldn't forget that, at least in the formulation of the Catholic Church, the natural law ultimately comes from their God. Like the divine command theory, natural law ethics is open to all of the objections of philosophical theology. Is there a God? Are there any significant proofs of this God's existence? Why is this God so *hidden*? How do we know our reason is sufficient to understand God's moral laws?

Moreover, a monotheistic natural law ethics must answer the challenge of the naturalistic fallacy. Why is the natural, good?

Whatever the conclusion, the gap between a non-teleological, factual, and scientific account of human nature and a teleological, ethical, and religious conception is a central dispute in modern culture. We don't know how to reconcile the two, or if one or the other is bankrupt. But, as the historian of philosophy W.T. Jones asserts in *A History of Western Philosophy*, "The whole history of philosophy since the seventeenth century is in fact hardly more than a series of variations on this central theme."

Chapter 6 - The Social Contract

The passions that incline [persons] to peace, are fear of death; desire of such things as are necessary to commodious living; and a hope by their industry to obtain them. And reason suggesteth convenient articles of peace, upon which [persons] may be drawn to agreement.
~ Thomas Hobbes

1. Hobbes and the Social Contract

Moving in western culture from the ancient and medieval periods into the sixteenth and seventeenth centuries, we approach modernity. The discovery of the new world, developments in commerce and industry, the Reformation, the scientific revolution, and the rise of the secular alongside the decline of Christianity transformed western civilization. Inevitably, natural law theory would be scrutinized. The major figures of the period, Rene Descartes (1596-1650), Benedict de Spinoza (1632-1677), John Locke (1632-1704) and Gottfried Leibniz (1646-1716), all tried to reconcile the new secular ideas with traditional Christian morality. But the most revolutionary of all the new theorists was Thomas Hobbes (1588-1679), who believed that ethical norms weren't to be found in a God's cosmic plan, but in our social and political agreements.

Hobbes detested violence. He had read Thucydides' account of the Peloponnesian War, and had personally witnessed the decades of English civil war which culminated with the beheading of Charles II. The desire to avoid war motivated both his moral and political thought. Hobbes' philosophy began by considering what the world would be like without morality. He believed that it would be *a state of nature;* a terrible place without art, literature, commerce, industry, or culture. Most terrifying of all, it would be a place of "continual fear and danger of violent death; and the life of [humans] solitary, poor, nasty, brutish, and short." But why would it be so bad?

In the first place, Hobbes believed that human beings endeavor desperately to fulfill their desires for food, clothing, shelter, power, honor, glory, comfort, pleasure, self-aggrandizement, and a life of ease. Unfortunately, such things are scarce. In addition, he believed that persons were relatively equal in their power. Given desires, scarcity, relative power equality, and the predominant sense of self-interest all human beings exhibit, Hobbes concluded that human beings, in a state of nature, would be engaged in a fierce struggle over scarce resources. Individuals would attack, steal, destroy and invade to protect themselves and prove their status. Thus, Hobbes' first thesis: *the state of nature is a state of war*.

Hobbes' second thesis was that *individuals in a state of nature have no a priori (natural, before experience) moral law that obligates them to constrain their behavior*. For Hobbes, self-preservation justified the use of force and fraud to defend ourselves in a state of nature. In this state, only the power of others limited what we can do. Hobbes called this *the right of nature*. But this state is antithetical to our survival, and so the desire for self-preservation expressed itself in Hobbes' third thesis: *fear of death and the desire for a good life incline us toward peace*. Hobbes called this *the law of nature*. Morality is defined by articles of peace, essentially, the rules to which any rational self-interested person would agree. The state of nature demands that we follow one of the two formulations of the self-preservation principle. In the state of nature, we should exercise our right of nature; in the state of peace, we should follow the law of nature. These laws of nature bear no resemblance to the medieval concept of natural law;

Chapter 6 - The Social Contract

they simply demand self-preservation. In other words, morality is the set of rules that make peaceful living possible.

This led to Hobbes' fourth thesis: *though it's in our own interest to agree to the articles of peace; it isn't rational to comply with our agreements unless some coercive power forces us*. Otherwise, we might feign agreement and, when the other complies, violate the accord. To prevent this, a coercive power must ensure that we comply with our agreements. This agreement between individuals to establish the laws that make communal living possible and an agency to enforce those laws is called the social contract.

2. A Theory of Morality

While issues surrounding the nature of the coercive agency which guarantees compliance with the social contract leads to political theory, the agreed-upon rules constitute morality. Morality is the agreed-upon, mutually advantageous conventions which, assuming others' compliance, make society possible. Thus, self-interest ultimately justifies morality. We can easily see that killing, lying, cheating, and stealing are prohibited since they threaten society and aren't in anyone's self-interest. Whether the moral prohibitions against things like homosexuality, prostitution, abortion, or euthanasia are justified in terms of individual and societal interest is more debatable.

But whatever the agreed-upon rules, according to the theory they don't exist prior to human contracts. We create morality by our agreements within the constraints demanded by self-preservation and self-interest; we don't discover antecedent moral truths. Prior to the contract, actions are neither moral nor immoral. But after the contract is signed, society forbids some actions, allows others, remains undecided on a few, and continually renegotiates the contract to satisfy rival parties. Therefore, the moral sphere is one of continual bargaining and power-struggling where conflict is resolved through moral discourse, a political mechanism, or violence. Hobbes' detested the latter option.

We conclude by noting that the social contract theory is especially attractive for a number of reasons. First, it takes the mystery out of ethics. Morality has to do with all of us being able to live well. Second, it gives us objective reasons why we shouldn't kill or lie, but there are no mysterious moral facts from on high. Third, moral rules aren't meant to interfere in people's lives. Fourth, it doesn't assume we are altruistic; it assumes we are self-interested, probably a more realistic assumption. And finally, it gives us a reason to be moral—morality is in our self-interest.

3. An Actual Contract

Following Hobbes, the contemporary Princeton philosopher Gilbert Harman (1938 -) argues that morality consists of the moral conventions to which self-interested persons have *actually* agreed. To support his thesis, he shows how this view explains many otherwise inexplicable moral puzzles. For example, why do we take the duty not to harm others to be greater than the duty to help them? Harman says this rule results from a real bargaining process between groups of unequal power. No group wants to be harmed, but the duty to help benefits the weakest groups. Since the weak are less powerful in the bargaining process, the rich and powerful dictate only a weak duty to help others. In that way, the rich and powerful can be protected from harm by a strong duty, but not inconvenienced by a strong duty to help others. Or consider that we have virtually no moral duties toward non-human animals. We can explain this easily if our moral relationships with animals arose through a bargaining process in which animals had no say. Thus, Harman contends, morality results from an actual contract between rational bargainers.

Chapter 6 - The Social Contract

But what happens when we reach an impasse in the bargaining process, or some moral puzzle appears incapable of resolution? Harman suggests that we begin by making explicit the role self-interest plays in moral bargaining. For example, the rich and powerful tend to emphasize freedom and property rights, while the poor and weak tend to emphasize equality. If self-interest was made more explicit, it would lend greater clarity and honesty to moral disputes.

More enigmatic moral disputes—say moral vegetarianism—revolve around principles other than self-interest. If moral rules are conventions, then we all must accept that we have no privileged moral status when it comes to morality. Consider then that vegetarians share principles that most others do not. Since we don't violate the self-interest of vegetarians by eating meat, vegetarians should be tolerant of our meat-eating practices, as we should be of their vegetarianism.

Similarly with abortion, if anti-abortionists admit they have no privileged access to the moral truth but accept principles that others don't, they will be inclined to be more tolerant. Of course, Harman admits abortion is a tough case and that anti-abortion sentiment might survive a convention that dictates otherwise. But eventually we will reach a compromise, one favoring the pro-choice side since self-interest plays a less significant role, Harman believes, for the pro-lifers. In other words, since morality is grounded ultimately in self-interest, moral rules that oppose people's interests will defer to more self-interested rules.

Harman's conclusion here exemplifies contractarian thinking; moral rules must be in an individual's self-interest and, if they are not, they won't ultimately survive because not enough individuals will be motivated to abide by them. In fact, the fundamental tenet of the contractarian approach to morality is that any rule of social constraint is an arbitrary imposition upon us unless everyone's compliance can be shown to promote one individual's preferences, concerns, interests, etc.

Of course, there are "unconditionally cooperative" individuals who will act altruistically whatever the cost, and abide by their agreements even when it isn't in their self-interest. However such individuals are in the minority. Thus religious, political, and familial institutions—as well as a number of philosophical arguments—have tried to convince persons to forego their self-interest for some greater good. Nevertheless, this has always been a difficult if not impossible task. Consider how difficult it is—even with an enforcement agency in place—to prevent individuals from pursuing their self-interest. People cheat on their taxes even with coercive enforcement in place. Perhaps morality would have a more firm foundation if we could demonstrate to everyone that moral rules are in their self-interest. And if moral rules can't satisfy this requirement, then we have no reason to follow them. This emphasis on harnessing, rather than repressing, self-interested behavior is the hallmark of the contractarian approach.

4. Morals By Agreement

Another contemporary philosopher who follows in the tradition of Hobbes is David Gauthier (1932 -), professor emeritus of the University of Pittsburgh. In his influential text, *Morals By Agreement*, he argues that *voluntary* compliance with moral rules, even in the absence of enforcement, is in one's self-interest. Specifically, he contends that one should become a constrained maximizer, a person disposed to cooperate with others on the condition that they expect those others to cooperate with them. We can all do better by voluntarily cooperating, considering the cost of establishing and maintaining enforcement agencies.

Chapter 6 - The Social Contract

Like Harman, Gauthier contends that bargaining may resolve contract disputes, and he advances a bargaining theory to support this claim. Unlike Hobbes and Harman, Gauthier's moral theory depends less heavily on self-interest. If morality and self-interest coincide, Gauthier claims, then morality would be easy; we would just follow our interests. But this seems to be mistaken since morality and self-interest so often conflict. Gauthier believes that morality calls upon us, at least sometime, to constrain ourselves from self-interested pursuits. On the other hand, if morality isn't self-interested, then you have no reason to be moral. It's from this paradox that morality derives.

What Gauthier has in mind echoes Hobbes' thinking. We must constrain ourselves to be moral, but because constraint allows us to live peacefully, it's ultimately self-interested. In the end, Gauthier agrees with both Harman and Hobbes that morality is grounded in self-interest and that moral constraint is the price we pay for a civilized society. But how exactly does Gauthier say that self-interest leads to morality?

To answer this question Gauthier develops his theory of morality as part of a theory of rational choice; in essence, morality is both self-interested and rational. We might begin by considering the conception of rationality central to his theory. For Gauthier, practical reason is strictly instrumental. This is sometimes called the *maximizing* notion of rationality. Accordingly, to be rational is to be disposed to act in a way that maximizes the satisfaction of one's interests, interests here are understood as one's considered, but nonetheless, subjectively determined preferences. On this conception of rationality, one's preferential interests need not be exclusively *in* the self, but preferential interests *of* the self, which may include interest in others.

The notion of rationality used here derives from that employed by economists in the classical tradition. The individual is the ultimate unit of analysis in this tradition. Individuals are assumed to make choices on the basis of their preferences and beliefs about the world. The choice is rational in this sense when it's consistent with those beliefs and preferences. Effects of human action and interaction are then explained as the intended or unintended outcomes of the individual choices producing them. As we will see, the effect of choices that are individually rational may be nonetheless collectively harmful but, at the same time, avoidable. In a nutshell, to avoid collectively harmful outcomes, we must adopt what Gauthier calls "morals by agreement," those principles we can all agree to for our mutual benefit. This is the essence of morality. To better understand what Gauthier is getting at we turn to the theory of games.

5. Game Theory and the Prisoner's Dilemma

For our purposes, a game is an interactive situation in which individuals, called players, choose strategies to deal with each other in attempting to maximize their individual utility. There are several ways of distinguishing games including: 1) in respect to the number of players involved; 2) in respect to the number of repetitions of play; 3) in respect of the order of the various player's preferences over the same outcomes. On the one extreme are games of pure conflict, so-called zero-sum games, in which players have completely opposing interests over possible outcomes. These would include games like chess and football. On the other extreme are games of pure harmony, so-called games of coordination. In the middle are games involving both conflict and harmony in respect of others—so-called mixed-motive games. One particular game interests us most—*the prisoner's dilemma*—since it

Chapter 6 - The Social Contract

describes the situation in Hobbes' state of nature, and is the central problem in contractarian moral theory.

The prisoner's dilemma is one of the most widely debated situations in game theory, and it has implications for a variety of human interactive situations. A prisoner's dilemma is an interactive situation in which it's better for all to cooperate rather than for no one to do so, yet it's best for each not to cooperate, regardless of what the others do.

In the story, two prisoners have committed a serious crime, but all of the evidence necessary to convict them isn't admissible in court. Both prisoners are held separately and are unable to communicate. The prisoners are called separately by the authorities and each offered the same proposition. Confess and if your partner does not, then you will be convicted of a lesser crime and serve one year in jail, while the unrepentant prisoner will be convicted of a more serious crime and serve ten years. If you don't confess and your partner does, then it's you who will be convicted of the more serious crime and your partner of the lesser crime. Should neither of you confess the penalty will be two years for each of you, but should both of you confess the penalty will be five years. In the following matrix, you are the row chooser and your partner the column chooser. The first number in each parenthesis represents the payoff for you in years in prison, the second number your partner's years. Let us assume each player prefers the least number of years in prison possible. In matrix form, the situation looks like this:

	Prisoner 2	
	Confess	Don't Confess
Prisoner 1 Confess	(5, 5)	(1, 10)
Don't Confess	(10, 1)	(2, 2)

So you reason as follows: If your partner confesses, you had better confess because if you don't you will get 10 years rather than 5. If your partner doesn't confess, again you should confess because you will only get 1 year rather than 2 for not confessing. So no matter what your partner does, you ought to confess. The reasoning is the same for your partner. The problem is that when both confess the outcome is worse for both than if neither had confessed. You both could have done better, and neither of you done worse if you had not confessed. You might have made an agreement not to confess, but this would not solve the problem. The reason is this: although agreeing not to confess is rational, compliance is not rational.

The prisoner's dilemma describes the situation that humans found themselves in Hobbes' state of nature. If the prisoners cooperate, they both do better; if they don't cooperate, they both do worse. But both have a good reason not to cooperate—they aren't sure the other will reciprocate. We can escape this dilemma, Hobbes maintained, by installing a coercive power that makes us comply with our agreements.

Chapter 6 - The Social Contract

But Gauthier argues for the rationality of voluntary non-coerced cooperation and compliance with agreements given the costs to each of us of enforcement agencies. Again Gauthier advocates that we accept "morals by agreement." Whether compliance with our moral and political agreements is in our self-interest without an enforcement mechanism is still a matter of dispute.

6. How Strong is Contract Theory?

But is it true that morality consists in a set of rules that rational, self-interested people agree to for their mutual benefit? Is that all there is to morality? There are a number of complications surrounding the social contract theory, but two objections are salient. *First*, some question the idea that humans are relative power equals, and *second* others argue that the theory can't account for our moral intuitions about so-called "weak rationals." We'll consider each objection in turn.

If humans aren't relatively equal in their power then ethics degenerates into "might makes right." What contract theorists mean by relative power equality is that no person or group of people can dominate another group for long without a successful uprising. At first glance, history seems to both confirm and deny the power equality assumption. On the one hand, dominated parties often arise and, through violence or renegotiation, revise social contracts. On the other hand, some groups have long been dominated without successful rebellion. This history of domination, slavery, and oppression of certain groups suggests that people may not be relative power equals, and this undermines the idea that contract theory can be squared with our ordinary moral intuitions. If the moral contract is drawn between unequal parties, then the more powerful parties will have an advantage.

The other related difficulty concerns "weak rationals," which includes children, non-human animals, the mentally disadvantaged, and others incapable of participating in or understanding a contract. (Others might be technological inferiors or what we might call "weak culturals.") Inasmuch as our ordinary moral intuitions suggest that we have obligations toward weak rationals, either the theory or our moral intuition is mistaken. Unless we can devise some way to reconcile contractarianism with our moral intuitions—that weak rationals and relative power unequals deserve moral consideration—then, assuming ordinary moral intuitions are reliable, contract theory is flawed.

A number of replies to the above objections have been advanced by contract theorists. First, some reply that those who are unequal in power don't deserve moral consideration. Perhaps it costs the society too much to take care of such people. (Won't almost all of us be weak rationals someday, simply by aging?) The argument to defend this thesis would be complex, but suffice it to say that most of us would dismiss such an argument. It's hard to take seriously a moral theory without some sense of compassion.

Another reply would modify contract theory. Since we must constrain our self-interest for the common good, perhaps it's a good idea to habituate the kinds of cooperative behaviors that make the social contract possible. If we were to treat weak rationals badly, then we might habituate socially destructive behaviors, rather than the cooperative behaviors that make social living possible. For example, according to contract theory, there is no good reason not to kick your dog if doing so makes you feel better. But in our modified contract theory, the reason not to act aggressively toward our dog would be that we might habituate that behavior, and then find that such behavior would not be in our self-interest when directed toward a relative power equal. Or perhaps weak rationals may not turn out to be so weak after all.

Chapter 6 - The Social Contract

7. A Veil of Ignorance

In further support of contract theory, we might look at the approach of the Harvard philosopher John Rawls whose book, *A Theory of Justice*, is probably the most influential philosophical ethics text of the past fifty years. Rawls' contractarian approach differs radically from that of either Gauthier or Harman because it finds its inspiration not in Hobbes, but in Locke, Rousseau, and Kant.

Rawls begins by considering the *original position* where parties deliberate about the rules of right conduct that will be universally applicable in society. In the bargaining position parties are impartial, that is, everyone's interest count equally. This is guaranteed by the so-called *veil of ignorance* that hides from contractors any knowledge of themselves. You don't know your race, sex, social class, or nationality from behind the veil of ignorance. Although parties are self-interested and want to establish rules beneficial for themselves, in reality, self-interest is ruled out by the veil of ignorance because from behind it one can't differentiate their interests from the interests of others.

The rules agreed to by rational bargainers behind a veil of ignorance are justifiable moral rules. This solution demonstrates a hypothetical way that contract theory could account for the rules favored by ordinary moral consciousness since the veil of ignorance assures us that impartial rules will result. However, by mitigating the role played by self-interest, this type of contract radically departs from the account of morality given by Hobbes or the neo-Hobbesians.

It's important to keep in mind that the agreement that stems from the original position is both hypothetical and non-historical. It's hypothetical in the sense that the principles to be derived are what the parties would, under certain legitimating conditions, agree to, not what they have agreed to. In other words, Rawls seeks to persuade us that the principles of justice that he derives are what we would agree upon if we were in the hypothetical situation of the original position. That is what gives those principles their moral weight. It's non-historical in the sense that it isn't supposed that the agreement has ever been entered into.

Rawls claims that the parties in the original position would adopt two such principles, which would then govern the assignment of rights and duties and regulate the distribution of social and economic advantages across society. First, *each person is to have an equal right to the most extensive scheme of equal basic liberties compatible with a similar scheme of liberties for others*. The basic liberties of citizens are, roughly speaking, political liberty (i.e., to vote and run for office); freedom of speech and assembly, liberty of conscience and freedom of thought, freedom of property; and freedom from arbitrary arrest. It's a matter of some debate whether freedom of contract can be inferred as being included among these basic liberties.

The first principle is more or less absolute, and may not be violated, even for the sake of the second principle, above an unspecified but low level of economic development. However, because various basic liberties may conflict, it may be necessary to trade them off against each other for the sake of obtaining the largest possible system of rights. There is thus some uncertainty as to exactly what is mandated by the principle, and it's possible that a plurality of sets of liberties satisfy its requirements.

The *second* principle is that social and economic inequalities are to be arranged so that:

a) They are to be of the greatest benefit to the least-advantaged members of society (the difference principle).

Chapter 6 - The Social Contract

b) Offices and positions must be open to everyone under conditions of fair equality of opportunity.

Rawls' claim in a) is that departures from equality regarding a list of what he calls primary goods—things all rational people want—are justified only to the extent that they improve the lot of those who are worst-off under that distribution in comparison with the previous, equal, distribution. His position is in some sense egalitarian, with a proviso that equality isn't to be achieved by worsening the position of the least advantaged.

An important consequence here is that inequalities can actually be just in Rawls's view, as long as they are to the benefit of the least well off. His argument for this position rests heavily on the claim that morally arbitrary factors (for example, the family we're born into) shouldn't determine our life chances or opportunities. Rawls' position is consistent with the intuition that we don't deserve inborn talents, thus we aren't entitled to all the benefits we could possibly receive from them, meaning that at least one of the criteria which could provide an alternative to equality in assessing the justice of distributions is eliminated.

The stipulation in b) requires not merely that offices and positions are distributed on the basis of merit, but that all have reasonable opportunity to acquire the skills on the basis of which merit's assessed. It's often thought that this stipulation, and even the first principle of justice, may require greater equality than the difference principle because large social and economic inequalities, even when they are to the advantage of the worst-off, will tend to seriously undermine the value of political liberties and any measures towards fair equality of opportunity.

8. Conclusion

In conclusion, it appears that contract theory is viable to the extent that individuals are relatively equal in power, and when the contract is continually and fairly renegotiated. But in the real world, this doesn't appear to be the case. We always seem to have an imperfect contract which represents the interests of the stronger, more concerned, or more persuasive parties. Whether an equilibrium can be reached in the bargaining process is problematic, inasmuch as individuals rarely encounter each other on a level playing field. So even though it may be the case that morality is, as Harman supposes, nothing more than the result of bargaining and power-struggling between various groups, we can still ask whether this should be the case. Shouldn't morality be more than just a contract between rational bargainers?

Still, let us also note how much of contemporary western civilization operates within a contract framework. We have contracts that govern our property, our mortgages, and our marriages. We have contracts that state who will speak for us if we can't speak for ourselves, and what kind of medical technology is deemed appropriate to sustain our lives. In short, we are a contract society. Whether this is for the better, only the reader can judge.

Finally, consider the conclusions about contract theory drawn by many philosophers. Contract theory, they say, answers the question of why "we" should be moral, but not why "I" should be moral. Concerning the latter question, why not be a free rider, someone who acts immorally when they can get away with it? It may be good collectively for us all to be moral, but individually it seems I do best by being immoral if I can get away with it. This may be the toughest question for contract theory. Hobbes' solution was to

Chapter 6 - The Social Contract

have the enforcement agency penalize the non-cooperative move in order to deter individuals from choosing it. But this raises the problem of corruption and injustice among the coercive agencies—governments and their law enforcement departments. And if there were a world government or even a galactic one to adjudicate our disputes, how can we assure that they won't be corrupt?

Perhaps then there will be no solution to the problem of how to get humans to cooperate until we change the hard-wiring of our brains.

Chapter 7 – Kant's Ethics

Nothing can possibly be conceived in the world ... which can be called good without qualification, except a good will.
~ Immanuel Kant

1. Kant and Hume

The German philosopher Immanuel Kant (1724-1804), called by many the greatest of modern philosophers, was the preeminent defender of deontological (duty) ethics. He lived such an austere and regimented life that the people of his town were reported to have set their clocks by the punctuality of his walks. He was an accomplished astronomer, mathematician, metaphysician, one of the most celebrated philosophers of all time and the crowning figure of the Enlightenment. The European Enlightenment celebrated the idea that human reason was sufficient to understand, the world. Perhaps the greatest rationalist ever, Kant also coined the motto of the Enlightenment: "dare to think."

To understand Kant, we might briefly consider his predecessor David Hume (1711-1776). Hume had awakened Kant "from his dogmatic slumber" as Kant put it, forcing him to reconsider all of his former beliefs. Hume's skepticism had challenged everything for which the Enlightenment stood; he was perhaps the greatest and most consistent skeptic the Western world had yet produced. He argued that Christianity was nonsense, that scientific knowledge was uncertain, that the source of sense experience was unknown, and that ethics was subjective.

Hume believed that moral judgments express our sentiments or feelings, and that morality was based upon an innate sympathy we have for our fellow human beings. If humans possess the proper sentiments, they were moral; if they lack such sympathies, they were immoral. Hume attacked authority and tradition—an attack characteristic of the Enlightenment—but without the Enlightenment's faith in reason. In particular, he criticized the view that morality was based upon reason which, according to Hume, can tell us about facts, but never tell us about values. In short, reason is practical; it determines the means to some end. But ends come from desires and sentiments, not from reason.

In vivid contrast to natural law theory, our ends, goals, and purposes depend upon our passions and, consequently, no passions are irrational. Hume made these points in a few famous passages: "Reason is, and ought only to be the slave of the passions … [and] … it isn't contrary to reason to prefer the destruction of the whole world to the scratching of my finger."

Hume's skepticism stunned Kant. If desire preceded reason, and our passions can't be irrational, then Enlightenment rationalism was dead. How then can we reestablish faith in reason? How can we show that some passions and inclinations are irrational? In his monumental work *The Critique of Pure Reason*, Kant attempted to elucidate the rational foundations of both the natural and mathematical sciences, thereby defending reason against Hume's onslaught. He then turned his attention to establishing a foundation for ethics in *The Critique of Practical Reason*. If morality is subjective, as Hume thought, then the concept of an objective moral law was a myth. And if no passions are irrational, then anything goes in morality. In essence, Kant needed to answer Hume's subjectivism and irrationalism by demonstrating the rational foundations of the moral law.

2. Freedom and Rationality

Kantian philosophy is enormously complex and obscure, yet his main ideas about ethics are relatively easy to grasp. His most basic presupposition is his belief in human freedom. While the natural world operates according to laws of cause and effect, he argued, the moral world operates according to self-imposed "laws of freedom." We may reconstruct one of his arguments for freedom as follows:

- Without freedom, morality isn't possible.
- Morality exists, thus
- Freedom exists.

The first premise follows if we consider how determinism undermines morality. (See chapter 2) The second premise Kant took as self-evident, and the conclusion follows logically from the premises. But where does human freedom come from? Kant believed that freedom came from rationality, and he advanced roughly the following argument to support this claim:

- Without reason, we would be slaves to our passions
- If we were slaves to our passions, we would not be free;
- Thus, without reason, we would not be free.

Together, we now have the basis upon which to cement the connection between reason and morality.

- Without reason, there is no freedom
- Without freedom, there is no morality, thus
- Without reason, there is no morality.

Chapter 7 – Kant's Ethics

Kant believed moral obligation derived from our free, rational nature. But how should we exercise our freedom? What should we choose to do?

3. Intention, Duty, and Consequences

Kant began his most famous work in moral philosophy with these immortal lines: "Nothing in the world—indeed nothing even beyond the world—can possibly be conceived which could be called good without qualification except a good will." For Kant, a good will freely conforms itself and its desires to the moral law. That is its duty. Nevertheless, the moral law doesn't force itself upon us; we must freely choose to obey it. For Kant, the intention to conform our free will to the moral law, and thereby do our duty, is the essence of morality.

The emphasis on the agent's intention brings to light another salient issue in Kant's ethics. So long as the intention of an action is to abide by the moral law, then the consequences are irrelevant. For instance, if you try valiantly to save someone from a burning building but are unsuccessful, no one holds you responsible for your failure because your intention was good. The reverse is also true. If I intend to harm you, but inadvertently help you, I am still morally culpable.

Kant gave his own example to dramatize the role intention played in morality. Imagine shopkeepers who would cheat their customers given the opportunity, but who don't cheat them only because it's bad for business. In other words, the shopkeepers do the right thing only because the consequences of doing so are good. If they could cheat their customers without any repercussions, they would do so. According to Kant, these shopkeepers aren't moral. On the other hand, shopkeepers who give the correct change out of a sense of duty are moral.

The emphasis on the agent's intention captures another important idea in deontology, the emphasis on the right over good. Right actions are done in accordance with duty; they don't promote values like happiness or the common good. Kant makes it clear that dutiful conduct doesn't necessarily make us happy. In fact, it often makes us unhappy! We should do the right thing because it's our duty, not because it makes us happy. If we want to be happy, he says, we should follow our instincts, since instinct is a better guide to happiness than reason.

But morality can't rest upon passions. If it did, morality would be both subjective and relative. For ethics to be objective, absolute, and precise—to be like the sciences—it needs to be based upon reason. Only the appeal to the objectivity of reason allows us to escape the subjectivity of the passions. In summary, a good will intends to do its duty by using reason to follow the moral law without consideration of the consequences.

4. Hypothetical and Categorical Imperatives

But what exactly does reason command? We have already seen how reason commands actions given antecedent desires. If we want a new car, then reason tells us the various means to achieve this end. We can save or borrow the money, pray, enter a raffle, call our mother, or steal a car. But whatever we do, reason only tells us how to pursue the end; it doesn't tell us which ends are worth pursuing. Commands or imperatives of this sort, Kant called *hypothetical imperatives*, since they depend upon some desires or interests that we happen, hypothetically, to have.

Kant distinguished between two types of hypothetical imperatives. The type we have been discussing so far, what he called "rules of skill," demand a definite means to a contingent (dependent) end. There are also what Kant called "counsels of

Chapter 7 – Kant's Ethics

prudence," which are contingent means to a definite end. Kant recognized that happiness was a common end or universal goal for all individuals, but that the means to this end was uncertain. For example, we may think that getting a new car or losing weight will make us happy, but when we get the new car or slimmer figure we may still be unhappy. Even though the end is definite, the means to the end aren't. Thus, there are no universal hypothetical imperatives because either the ends are contingent or the means to the end are uncertain.

But does reason command anything absolutely? In other words, does reason issue any imperatives which don't depend on contingent ends or uncertain means? Hume had claimed that reason didn't command in this way and that any rational commands depend upon our passions. But if absolute commands exist—commands independent of personal taste—then the essence of the moral law will be revealed.

Now when we think about any law in general, we recognize immediately that law is characterized by its universal applicability. So that, if relativity theory is true, then time is relative to motion everywhere throughout the universe. Similarly, the distributive law of mathematics applies no matter what numbers we insert into it or what planet we are on. Kant believed that the moral law was like this. If there really is a reason why for example killing innocent people is wrong, then the reason this is so applies universally. It doesn't matter that we want, desire, or like to kill innocent persons; we still violate the moral law if we follow this desire.

Of course, we can say that killing innocent people doesn't violate the moral law, just as we can say that time isn't relative to motion, or that the distributive law works only on Monday. But our statements don't affect these laws; rather, the laws determine the truth of our statements. Kant held that a universally applicable moral law governs human behavior and can be discovered by human reason.

Kant had seized upon the idea of universalization as the key to the moral law. He called the first and most famous formulation of the moral law *the categorical imperative*: "Act only according to that maxim by which you can at the same time will that it should become a universal law." A maxim is a subjective principle of action which reveals our intention. To universalize a maxim is simply to ask, "what if everybody did this?" We should act according to a principle which we can universalize with consistency or without inconsistency. By testing the principle of our actions in this way, we determine if they are moral. If we can universalize our actions without any inconsistency, then they are moral; if we can't do so, they are immoral. For examples, there is no logical inconsistency in universalizing the maxim, whenever we need a car we will work hard to earn the money; however, there is something inconsistent about universalizing the maxim, whenever we need a car we will steal it. And that problem is that there is something logically inconsistent about a world in which everyone steals cars. (More on this in a moment.)

Another famous formulation was: "Act so that you treat humanity, whether in your own person or in that of another, always as an end and never merely as a means." This formulation introduces the idea of respect for persons. Individuals aren't a means to an end; we shouldn't use people. Instead, people are ends in themselves with their own goals and purposes. Whether we use ourselves or others, we violate the imperative if we treat any human being without dignity and respect. Certainly, it's true that we all use people to an extent. We use physicians, teachers, nurses, and auto mechanics to get what we want. But there is a difference between paying persons for services and using them *merely* as a

Chapter 7 – Kant's Ethics

means to your end. In the latter case, we disregard their inherent worth.

The categorical imperative commands actions in two different ways. It specifically forbids or requires certain actions, and it commands that certain general goals be pursued. The former are called perfect duties, the latter imperfect duties. *Perfect duties* include: don't lie, don't kill innocent persons, and don't use people. We should never perform these actions. *Imperfect duties* include: helping others, developing our talents, and treating others with respect. These duties are absolute, but the way we satisfy them varies. There is flexibility in how we help others, treat them with respect, or develop our talents. When we universalize a maxim that violates a perfect duty, we will an inconsistent world. When we universalize a maxim that violates an imperfect duty, we will an unpleasant world.

5. Kant's Examples

Kant provided four examples—making false promises, committing suicide, developing our talents, and helping others—to demonstrate how the categorical imperative governs human conduct. Consider Kant's first example, making a false promise. Can we consistently will the principle, "whenever in need of money, make a false promise to get it?" We can't, since a world where everyone acts according to this maxim would be inconsistent. Why? In such a world: 1) false promises would be useful because there would be persons to believe them; and 2) false promises would not be useful because, in a short time, nobody would believe them. Such a world isn't even possible. On the one hand, it would contain the necessary preconditions for false promises to be successful—people to believe our lies—and, on the other hand, the normal and predictable result of universal false promising would be that no lies would be believed. So it isn't just that this world is unpleasant; it's logically impossible.

Consider Kant's second example. Imagine that we are depressed and contemplate suicide. Our principle of action is "whenever we are depressed we will commit suicide." Now try to universalize a world in which everyone does this. What would it be like? In such a world: 1) people would exist to commit suicide; and 2) people would not exist to commit the suicides they intend. Such a world isn't logically possible. On the one hand, it would contain the necessary preconditions of suicide—live people to commit the act—and, on the other hand, the normal and predictable result of universal suicide would be that everyone would be dead. It's easy to think of other examples. Worlds, where everyone were killers or bank robbers, would be logically impossible in the same way. Kant had demonstrated, at least to his own satisfaction, that these actions were both immoral and irrational.

If we consider the same two actions—making false promises and suicide—in terms of the second formulation of the categorical imperative, we discover that they violate it as well. If we make a false promise to someone, then we use that person as a means to our end. Analogously, if we commit suicide, then we use ourselves to achieve some end. When universalization of a maxim is inconsistent or when we use ourselves or others, we violate perfect duties. Kant believed that telling the truth and not committing suicide exemplify perfect duties. There are no exceptions to them.

Kant also believed we have a moral obligation to develop our talents, which was his third example. Suppose we are comfortable and prefer to indulge ourselves rather than develop our talents. We act according to this maxim: "since we are reasonably well-off, we won't develop our talents." Upon reflection, we recognize that failure to develop our talents violates a duty and can't be

Chapter 7 – Kant's Ethics

universalized consistently, for if everyone failed to develop their natural talents, they would not fulfill the purpose for which those talents exist.

He might have added that nothing useful would be accomplished in human society without the development of talent. Yet, Kant never claimed such a world was impossible, unimaginable, or logically inconsistent. Rather, rational persons can't will this maxim to be a universal law without disastrous and unpleasant results.

Similarly, we have a moral obligation to help others, Kant's fourth example. Suppose we are prosperous and care little for others. We violate a duty by not helping others, and we can't universalize the maxim, for we may need the benefit of others in the future. Again, Kant didn't say this world was impossible, but he also didn't think any rational person desired such a world.

If we consider the same two actions—developing our talents and helping others—in terms of the second formulation of the categorical imperative, we discover similar difficulties. When universalization of a maxim has disastrous results or when we fail to treat ourselves and others as ends, we violate imperfect duties. Therefore, developing our talents and helping others are imperfect duties. They are absolute duties, but the specific means by which we satisfy these duties are open.

We may say that the categorical imperative is the formal representation of the moral law to the human mind. It commands human conduct independent of context. Compare the categorical imperative, as an abstract formulation of the moral law, to the distributive law in mathematics. This law states: $a(b+c) = ab+ac$. As stated, the principle is merely formal and without content. We give it content by putting numbers into the equation. The categorical imperative functions similarly in the moral domain.

Philosophical Ethics: Theory And Practice

There, we place the maxim that operates in the moral context (situation) into the formulation to determine what to do. When we want to steal a library book or trash the sidewalk we ask, "what if everybody did this?" Recognizing the negative implications of our maxim, we see how it violates the categorical imperative. Theoretically, we may place any principle into the formulation to determine its morality. Those who don't test their maxim in this manner, turn away from the moral law.

6. Problems with Universalization

Despite its initial plausibility, universalization is problematic. For one thing, it's easy to universalize immoral maxims. Suppose we act according to the maxim, "Catholics should be exterminated." There is no problem universalizing this maxim, in fact, we hope it does become universal if we really hate Catholics. The maxim "always kill Catholics," just like the maxim "never kill Catholics," can be universalized without contradiction by consistent Catholic-haters. Therefore, the test for universalization can't discriminate between the two actions. We can also universalize a non-moral action like, "whenever you are alone, you should sing." We may universalize this without contradiction, but that doesn't mean it's moral.

It's also easy enough to think of non-moral or supposedly moral maxims which can't be universalized. We can't universalize maxims like, "whenever hungry, go to Sue's diner," or "whenever we want to go to our school, go!" It isn't possible for everyone to go Sue's diner or to our school. More significantly, many moral actions can't be universalized. We can't universalize the maxim, "sell all you have and follow the Lord." For if everyone is selling, no one is buying! We can't even universalize a simple maxim like: "put other people first," since everyone can't be last. So the test for universalization doesn't seem to adequately distinguish moral from immoral actions.

This brings to light a related difficulty. What maxim should we test for universalization? Maxims vary according to their generality or specificity. Kant tested very general maxims for universalization like: "We can't lie to achieve an end." Suppose we made the maxim more specific: "We can't lie except to save innocent people from murder." This maxim is universalizable and spares us from telling the truth to inquiring murderers who ask the whereabouts of their intended victims. We could make the maxim even more specific. "We can't lie except to save innocent people from murder and to spare people's feelings."

The problem is that as maxims become more specific, more questionable maxims become capable of consistent universalization. Eventually, we would be testing very specific maxims. Suppose a bald philosopher professor, Horatio Rumpelstiltskin, was about to steal a book from the college library on Thursday at 12:22 p.m. He would discover, upon careful examination, that he could universalize a world where all so named and described individuals stole books at precisely that time. If maxims become this specific, universalization has no meaning. Thus, maxims must have some generality to be properly tested.

Now suppose I test the following maxim. "We can't lie except to achieve our ends." This maxim is sufficiently general to be universalized, but not sufficiently specific to rule out immoral actions. And the problem isn't ameliorated by turning to the second formulation of the imperative. Does respect for persons tell us anything about whether we should universalize general or specific maxims? Should I always respect persons, or always respect them except in certain situations? It appears that universalization isn't as simple as it initially appeared.

7. General Difficulties

Kant claimed that duties are absolute. But if duties are absolute, then what about conflicts between duties? Kant stated that perfect duties supersede imperfect ones, and thus the duty not to lie precedes the duty to help others. If this is so, it follows that we must tell the truth to inquiring murderers. (This was Kant's own example.) But this example presented great difficulties for Kant. Surely duties have exceptions and even perfect duties aren't sacrosanct. Surely you should lie to an inquiring murderer. Kant might have avoided this difficulty, as we have seen, by advocating that we universalize maxims with exceptions. A maxim like, "never lie except to inquiring murderers," isn't problematic.

Along these lines, the twentieth-century philosopher W.D. Ross (1877 – 1971) argued that no duties were absolute. Ross tried to modify Kant's theory to account for conflict of duty cases. According to Ross, we have prima facie—at first glance—duties, but they are conditional. Our actual duties depend upon the situation. In conflict of duty cases, we carefully weigh our duties and then proceed to do the best we can. The problem is whether Ross' conception of duties is too subjective and situational since individuals decide which duties apply in given situations. The main problem with Ross' version of deontology is its emphasis on subjects and situations, an emphasis Kant wanted to avoid.

Another problem with Kant's system is that it's so formal and abstract it hardly motivates us. Even if Kant could prove that ethics were completely rational, wouldn't this take something away from the importance of moral choice? Isn't ethics too messy and imprecise for the formal precision of Kant's system? Aristotle said that ethics could never be so precise, so maybe Kant demanded too much precision from his ethics.

Chapter 7 – Kant's Ethics

Another general difficulty is Kant's rejection of the importance of consequences. According to Kant, if we do our duty we are absolved of all responsibility for the consequences of our action. He defends this view in part because he believes we can never know the consequences of our actions with certainty. This is true to an extent, but this view rests upon very pessimistic assumptions about our knowledge of the consequences of our actions. If for no apparent reason we tell our friend she looks positively awful, we can be pretty sure she will feel bad about this. We are hardly absolved by our claim that we weren't sure she would feel bad. So sometimes we can be reasonably sure of the consequences of our actions, in which case duty may not be important. Much trouble has been caused by people who were simply "doing their duty."

8. Kant's Fundamental Idea

Despite the nuances connected with the idea of universalization, there is a core idea at the heart of Kant's theory which is his lasting legacy. We have all been reprimanded by someone saying "how would you like someone to do that to you?" And *this is Kant's fundamental idea*. If there is a reason why you don't want people to do something to you, then that same reason applies to what you want to do to others. It gives you a reason not to treat others in a way that you don't want to be treated. And, if you ignore that reason, you are acting irrationally.

This is the kind of rational constraint Kant believed imposed itself upon our conduct. Of course, we have all experienced people who believe that the rules that apply to us don't apply to them and, if they are bigger or more powerful than we are, there isn't much we can do. They might say, "You help me move on Saturday, but I won't help you move next week." We feel that they are doing something unfair and inconsistent, whether or not they recognize it. That is Kant's basic idea. A reason for one is a reason for all.

This purely rational morality is a fascinating idea. We saw in an earlier chapter how moral judgments might be truths of reason. Whether this is true depends upon our understanding of concepts like rationality, interests, and individuality. In the strong conception of rationality, others' interests give us a reason to act. In the weak conception, others' interests don't give us a reason. This issue also relates to the earlier discussion of egoism between Kalin and Medlin. If we think other people should respect our interests, so the argument goes, then we should respect theirs. But when we say others should respect our interests does that mean: 1) we want them to respect our interests; or 2) they have a reason to respect our interests. Kant and his contemporary followers argue for "2," while other philosophers argue for "1." Clearly, we want others to act in our interest, but it isn't clear our interests give others a reason to act.

A conception of individualism is also relevant. If we have a strong conception of individuality—one in which individuals are radically separate—it's hard to see how the other's interests or wants give us a reason to do anything. On the other hand, if we have a weak conception of individuality—one in which individuals are intimately connected—it's easy to see how the other's interests give us reason to act. Maybe the rise of individualism lessens our sense of obligation toward others, or maybe communalism lessens our sense of obligation toward ourselves. Whatever our conclusions, the conceptions of rationality, interests, and individuality play a significant role in determining whether Kant's primary idea is convincing for us.

Kant's basic idea is that morality is grounded in reason. If there really is a reason to treat people with dignity and respect, or not to lie or cheat them, then this reason applies to all of us whether we want it to or not. To say there are universal moral reasons

Chapter 7 – Kant's Ethics

ultimately confirms our belief in the intelligibility of reality. And, if the moral universe is unintelligible, then nothing matters.

9. Conclusion

Finally, despite all the positive contributions of Kant's moral thought, one final difficulty plagues the theory. Kant argued that the life of duty is the *only* truly good life. But there have been many decent and happy lives that weren't motivated by duty. Consider also persons who live from a sense of duty, but who are miserable and unhappy. They live without love, compassion, pleasure, beauty, or intellectual stimulation. Are such individual's moral exemplars? True, many live decadent lives in pursuit of pleasure or happiness while dismissing moral virtue. But Kant's ethics suffer from its emphasis on duty and virtue while neglecting happiness and pleasure. And if a philosophy stresses duty over happiness, then why should we do our duty? Duty may be part of morality, but so is happiness. With these considerations in mind, we now turn to a moral theory which emphasizes the good over the right, happiness over duty. That theory is utilitarianism.

Chapter 8 - Utilitarianism

...the Greatest Happiness Principle, holds that actions are right in proportion as they tend to promote happiness, wrong as they tend to produce the reverse of happiness. ~ John Stuart Mill

1. Utility and Happiness

Jeremy Bentham (1748 – 1832), who lived in London during the Industrial Revolution, was a philosopher and social reformer who wished to alleviate the period's dreadful living conditions. Poverty, disease, overcrowding, child labor, lack of sanitation, and miserable prison and factory conditions inspired Bentham to be an agent of social reform. He graduated from Oxford at the age of fifteen and used his prodigious gifts as a social critic and legal and constitutional reformer. He became the leader of a group of individuals, including James Mill (1773 – 1836) and John Stuart Mill (1806 – 1873), who espoused the principles of a moral philosophy called *utilitarianism*. Utilitarianism was an influential force in eighteenth and nineteenth-century England, and Bentham personally influenced the British legislature to adopt virtually all of his proposals.

The guiding principle of Bentham's thought was the principle of utility: human actions and social institutions should be judged right or wrong depending upon their tendency to promote the pleasure or happiness of the greatest number of people. A popular formulation of the principle is "promote the greatest happiness for the greatest number." Bentham himself defined the principle of utility as "*that principle which approves or disapproves of every action whatsoever, according to the tendency which it appears to have to augment or diminish the happiness of the party whose interest is in question.*" Bentham wasn't clear as to whether the principle

Chapter 8 - Utilitarianism

referred to the utility of individual actions or classes of actions, but he was clear "the party whose interest is in question" refers to "anything that can suffer." Thus, utilitarianism was the first moral philosophy to give a significant place to nonhuman animals.

Utility measures the happiness or unhappiness that results from a particular action. The net utility measures the balance of the happiness over the unhappiness or, in other words, the balance of an action's good and bad results. To compute the net utility, we subtract the unhappiness caused by an action from the happiness it causes. If an action produces more happiness than unhappiness—a positive net utility results. If it produces more unhappiness than happiness—a negative net utility results.

When deciding upon a course of action utilitarians take the following steps. First, they determine the available courses of action. Second, they add up all the happiness and unhappiness caused by each action. Third, they subtract the unhappiness from the happiness of each action resulting in the net utility. Finally, they perform that action from the available alternatives which has most net utility. (This is "act" utilitarianism, to be distinguished from another type shortly.)

If all of the available actions produce a positive net utility, or if some produce positive and some produce negative net utility, utilitarians perform the action that produces the most positive utility. If all the available actions produce a negative net utility, then they perform the one with the least negative utility. In summary, utilitarians perform that action which produces the greatest balance of happiness over unhappiness from the available alternatives. Thus, the first key concept of utilitarianism is that of maximizing utility or happiness.

It's important to note that computations of the net utility count everyone's happiness equally. Unlike egoists, who claim that persons should maximize their own utility, utilitarians don't place their own happiness above that of others. For example, egoism recommends that we insult others if that makes us happy, but utilitarianism does not. For utilitarians, the happiness we experience by insulting them is more than balanced by the injury they endure. Analogously, robbing banks, killing people, and not paying our taxes may make us happy, but these actions decrease the net utility. Therefore, utilitarianism doesn't recommend any of them.

Utilitarianism is a doctrine which grips the imagination of most twentieth-century people. Nearly all newspaper columnists, politicians, social reformers, and ordinary citizens believe that we should "make the world a better place," "increase social justice," "promote the general welfare," "establish equality," or "create the greatest happiness for the most people." Utilitarian thinking underlies most of these phrases, and many individuals believe they are morally obligated to increase the happiness and decrease the unhappiness in the world.

2. The Consequences

The next key concept of utilitarianism is that we judge moral actions by the *consequences* they produce. The only thing that counts in morality is the happiness and unhappiness produced by an action. In other words, according to utilitarianism, the ends justify the means. It doesn't matter how you do it, as long as you increase the net utility. In most cases, as we have already mentioned, the action that utilitarians recommend mimics the recommendations of other moral theories. For instance, given the choice of telling Sue that she looks beautiful or terrible, we would usually maximize utility by telling her the former. Similarly, given the choice of granting or denying her request for a loan, we would usually maximize utility by granting her request. However, if she

Chapter 8 - Utilitarianism

will probably use the money to buy drugs, become intoxicated and then beat her children, we should deny her request. On the other hand, if Bob will use our money to feed his children, we should probably loan it to him. We should always perform that action that will, most likely, increase the happiness and decrease the misery of all involved.

Since the right action depends upon our assessment of the consequences, we must know what the consequences of our actions will be. Some object that the theory fails precisely because this isn't possible. And it's true that we never know absolutely what will happen as a consequence of our action. We may think the consequence of loaning Bob some money will be to cheer him up, but he might buy a gun and commit suicide! We may think the consequence of shooting Sue will be to hurt or kill her. But her subsequent paralysis might serve as the motivation for a successful writing career! In fact, any of our minuscule choices might alter human history, but we are only responsible for consequences we can reasonably anticipate. We anticipate the consequences as best we can and proceed to act accordingly. Thus, the fact that we can never be absolutely certain of the consequences of an act doesn't undermine utilitarianism.

We can now summarize our discussion thus far. Moral actions are those that produce the best consequences. The best consequences are those that have the most net utility, in other words, those that increase happiness and decrease unhappiness. When calculating the net utility everyone's interests count equally. The two key concepts of utilitarianism are happiness and consequences.

3. Examples of Utilitarian Reasoning

Consider this complex situation. Our teacher arrives the first day of class and makes the following announcement. "Let's not have class all semester! We will not inform the authorities, and we will keep it a secret. None of us will do any work. I will not have to teach, and you don't have to study. I will give you each an 'A' and you can give me excellent teaching evaluations. All of us will be happy, and the net utility increased. Class dismissed!" On the one hand, the action appears to maximize utility. No one has to work and no one is hurt. On the other hand, consider that the students are nursing students who need to learn the class material in order to function as competent nurses. If they don't learn the material, they will more likely be incompetent nurses, and a society of incompetent nurses decreases the net utility. Therefore, in this case, canceling class decreases net utility.

Note again how utilitarianism differs from egoism. If the teacher and the students were egoists, and would rather skip class than work, there would be no class. On the contrary, utilitarians assume that the net utility decreases if no teaching and learning take place. Remember, utilitarians usually prescribe exactly what other moral theories do. They forbid killing, lying, cheating, and stealing and prescribe helping others, working hard, and doing good deeds.

However, there are times when utilitarianism prescribes more controversial actions. Consider euthanasia. The natural law tradition, which has exerted more influence on Western ethics than any other, maintains that it's wrong to intentionally kill innocent persons even if they are suffering. But suppose Joe Smith is terminally ill, in excruciating pain, and asks his wife, his trusted comrade of fifty years, to kill him. Since he is more affected by his

Chapter 8 - Utilitarianism

illness than anyone else, it's reasonable to assume the net utility will increase by his death. There will be unhappiness caused by his death—his wife will mourn—but she would rather he die than suffer.

According to the utilitarian, if his wife kills him as he requests, she does the moral thing. This analysis also applies if he kills himself, or has his physician assist him. Here is a case in which what many of us believe to be immoral is, on a utilitarian analysis, perfectly acceptable. In this case, the pain and suffering of the relevant parties determine the proper course of action for a utilitarian.

Examine some other controversial cases. Many cultures have practiced infanticide, the willful killing of innocent children. Often their rationale was that the lack of available food for all children required that the youngest and most dependent be sacrificed for the group. On a utilitarian analysis, this is perfectly acceptable because one death is preferable to many. The same kind of thinking might have justified the use of atomic weapons in World War II. Assuming the choice was between "x" number of deaths as a result of dropping atomic bombs, and "4x" number of deaths as a result of a land invasion of Japan by American troops, the utilitarian choice was clear. (This is almost certainly historically inaccurate.)

If other options were available that had a greater net utility, say dropping the bomb in an unpopulated field as a show of force, then that action should have been performed. We may object that in the case of infanticide or atomic bombs, *innocence* has a moral significance which overrides the utilitarian conclusion. But, according to the utilitarian, maximizing utility determines the proper action.

4. Mill and Utilitarianism

John Stuart Mill, a protégé of Bentham and Mill's father James Mill, became the most eloquent spokesman for utilitarianism. Mill was a child prodigy; he studied Greek and mathematics from the age of three, and he had read all of Plato's dialogues in Greek by his early teens. Mill's classic work, *Utilitarianism*, sets forth the major tenets of the doctrine and reformulates many of Bentham's ideas.

In Chapter 2 of Utilitarianism, Mill noted that utilitarianism had concentrated upon the quantity of pleasure, but it didn't address any qualitative differences in pleasure. Mill feared the emphasis on pleasure would reduce utilitarianism to hedonism, a doctrine he considered "worthy of swine." He argued that some pleasures are qualitatively better than others, that the "higher" mental pleasures are superior in quality to the "lower" physical pleasures. How do we know this? Those who have experienced both kinds of pleasure show a decided preference for the higher ones, Mill stated, and this demonstrates that the higher pleasures are preferable. But are they really?

Mill admitted that nonhuman animals sometimes appear happier than human beings, but this is misleading. To paraphrase his famous quote: better an unhappy human than a happy pig; better a dissatisfied Socrates than a satisfied fool. If the fool or pig disagree, Mill continued, it's only because they haven't experienced higher pleasures. The major difficulty with Mill's view was its appeal to a standard other than happiness in order to make a distinction between kinds of happiness. But if there is another value besides happiness, then we have abandoned the idea that happiness is the only good.

Chapter 8 - Utilitarianism

In Chapter 4 of *Utilitarianism*, Mill began by defining the desirable end of all human endeavors. The only thing desirable is happiness, and all other valuable things are only means to the end of happiness. Bentham had wavered as to whether happiness or pleasure was the only good. In this more lucid version, happiness replaced pleasure as the moral standard. In this way, Mill avoided the charge that utilitarianism is hedonism in disguise.

Mill then proceeded to offer his famous "proof" of utilitarianism. We prove that something is visible by the fact that people see it, and we prove that something is audible by the fact that people hear it. In the same way "the sole evidence it's possible to produce that anything is desirable, is that people do actually desire it." For Mill, the simple fact that people desire happiness establishes it as desirable.

Of course merely because people desire happiness, the opponents of Mill replied, doesn't show that it's the only desirable thing. Mill answered that other goods like virtue or wealth are really means to happiness. But his opponents pointed to another difficulty with Mill's proof. It rests upon a confusion between what people *do* desire, and what they *ought* to desire. There mere fact that people actually desire happiness doesn't show, so critics of utilitarianism maintained, that happiness really should be desired. But Mill maintained that no other proof of the desirability of happiness was possible than to point out the fact that humans naturally desire it.

Mill also makes it clear that only the consequences matter. You do the right thing by saving your friends from drowning whether you do it for love or money. Why, Mill wonders, should we do our duty if it makes us unhappy? Amarillo Slim, a famous professional poker player, expressed Mill's position succinctly when he replied to someone who criticized his occupation: "Would the world really be better off if I was miserable pumping gas?"

5. Act and Rule Utilitarianism

Let us now turn to the question of whether utilitarians consider individual actions or classes of actions when deciding to maximize utility. Neither Bentham nor Mill addressed this question, but contemporary philosophers have made a distinction between two types of utilitarians. Act utilitarians ask "which individual action, from the available alternatives, maximizes utility?" Rule utilitarians ask "which rule, when generally adopted, maximizes utility?" Oftentimes there is no difference between the prescriptions of the two types of utilitarians; at other times, there is a great difference. We will illustrate this basic difference with a number of examples.

Imagine that we are stopped at a red traffic light at three in the morning. Looking both ways as far as possible down the road we are about to cross, we see no cars in sight. It suddenly occurs to us that we shouldn't remain stopped. Why? Because by running the red light we will save our mother a few minutes worry by getting home sooner, the country a little gas and pollution, and ourselves a little annoyance. Furthermore, we will get home sooner rather than later, decreasing the possibility that we or others will be injured in an accident. The net utility will be increased by our action and so, according to an act utilitarian, we should do it.

Contemplate another example. The President of the United States has requested that we turn down our thermostats to save heating oil. Unfortunately, our grandmother's arthritis is aggravated by a cold apartment. We reason as follows: if grandmother keeps her heat high, she will not contribute significantly to the country's oil problem. Moreover, she will feel much better and so will we. She will be more comfortable physically, and we will not have to listen to her complain about arthritis, government corruption, or greedy oil companies. Her physical state positively affects her mood. Her

Chapter 8 - Utilitarianism

good mood makes us and our family happier. An act utilitarian advises grandmother to keep her heat on high.

Finally, ponder this simple case. The sign on the college lawn says "keep off the grass." Officials at the college have determined that the college looks better, and attracts more students, with nice lawns. Now suppose you are in a hurry to complete some task that will make you and others happier, assuming that you complete it sooner rather than later. Assume also that cutting across the lawn saves a significant amount of time. Again, act utilitarians reason that their little footprints don't make a significant difference in the appearance of the college lawn, and since we can make other people happy by cutting across the lawn and completing our task sooner rather than later, we should do so.

Now consider these three cases from a rule utilitarian perspective. In every case, the rule utilitarian asks, "what if we made a general rule of these actions?" In other words, "what if everybody did these?" (This is the Kantian question, but Kant wants to know about the consistency, not the consequences, of rules.) Rule utilitarians want to know if rules maximize utility or bring about good consequences. Take the first case. It should be clear that if everyone disobeys traffic lights the consequences are disastrous. Given the choice between a rule that states "always obey traffic lights," or one that says "sometimes obey traffic lights," the first rule, not the second one, maximizes utility. Rule utilitarians argue that the net utility will decrease if persons are more selective about their obedience to rules. They might begin to disobey traffic lights at 11 p.m., whenever there are no cars in sight, or whenever they think they can beat the oncoming cars!

A comparable analysis applies in the other two cases. The rule, "don't turn up your thermostat to save heat for the country" maximizes utility compared with the rule, "turn up your thermostat if you're cold despite what the President requests." Similarly, the rule "don't walk on the grass" maximizes utility compared with the rule, "don't walk on the grass except when you are in a hurry." Therefore, in all of these cases act and rule utilitarians prescribe different actions. Act utilitarians perform the action that maximizes the utility, rule utilitarians act in accordance with the rule that, when generally adopted, maximizes utility. They both believe in maximizing utility, but they are divided as to whether the principle of utility applies to individual acts or general rules.

The issue between act and rule utilitarians revolves around the question, "is the moral life improved by practicing selective obedience to moral rules?" Act utilitarians answer in the affirmative; rule utilitarians answer it negatively. Rule utilitarians believe the moral life depends upon moral rules without which the net utility decreases. Act utilitarians believe that whether moral rules are binding or not depends upon the situation. Thus, act utilitarians treat moral rules as mere "rules of thumb," general guidelines open to exceptions, while rule utilitarians regard moral rules as more definitive. We will look at problems for both formulations of utilitarians in a moment. Let us now look at the most general problems for utilitarianism.

6. The Problems with Happiness

A *first* difficulty with using happiness as the moral standard is that the concept of the net utility implies that happiness and unhappiness are measurable quantities. Otherwise, we can't determine which actions produce the greatest net utility. Bentham elaborated a "hedonistic calculus" which measured different kinds of happiness and unhappiness according to their intensity, duration, purity, and so on. Some say that it's impossible to attach precise numerical values to different kinds of happiness and unhappiness. For example, it may be impossible to assign a numerical value to

Chapter 8 - Utilitarianism

the happiness of eating ice cream compared to the happiness of reading Aristotle. Still, we can prefer one to the other, say ice cream to Aristotle, and, therefore, we don't need precise numerical calculations to reason as a utilitarian.

A *second* difficulty is that it may be impossible to have "interpersonal" comparisons of utility. Should we give Sue our Aristotle book, or Sam our ice cream? Does Sue's reading pleasure exceed Sam's eating pleasure? There is no doubt that different things make different people happy. For some, reading and learning is an immense joy, for others, it's an exceptional ordeal. But we can still maximize utility. We should both give Sue the book and Sam the ice cream if possible, or if we can only do one or the other, we make our best judgment as to which choice maximizes utility. Besides, we agree about many of the things that make us happy and unhappy. Everyone is happy with some wealth, health, friends, and knowledge. Everyone is unhappy when they are in pain, hungry, tired, thirsty, and the like. We don't need precise interpersonal comparisons of utility to reason as a utilitarian.

Despite Mill's proof of utilitarianism, a *third* difficulty concerns doubts about the overriding value of happiness. Is it more valuable than, for example, freedom or friendship? Would we sacrifice these for the net utility? We would maximize utility by dropping "happiness pills" into everyone's drinks, but this doesn't mean we should do it. Shouldn't individuals be free to be unhappy? And if we believe this, isn't that because we think freedom is a value independent of happiness? We might refuse to take happiness pills even if given the choice because they limit the freedom to be unhappy.

Or suppose we promise to meet a friend but, in the meantime, some little children ask us to play with them. It may be that playing with the children maximizes utility. After all, our friend is popular and will probably make other arrangements after waiting a while. But maybe we should keep our promise. Maybe promise keeping or the friendship it engenders are valuable independent of the total happiness. These examples suggest that happiness isn't the only value.

Most contemporary utilitarians have abandoned the idea that happiness is the only value. They have retreated from claims about absolute values to claims about individual preferences. The type of utilitarianism which argues that we should maximize an individual's subjective preferences is called preference utilitarianism. The problem with this type of utilitarianism is that some subjective preferences might be evil.

A *fourth* difficulty is that utilitarianism considers only the quantity of utility and not its distribution. Should you give $100 to one needy person or $10 each to ten needy persons? The second alternative might be better even if the first one creates the most utility. Concerns with the total happiness have troubled many commentators, and some have suggested that we consider the "average utility."

But this version has problems too. Do we want a society where the average income is very high, say $1,000,000, but many people live in destitute poverty, or one where the average income is much lower, say $30,000, but no poverty exists? In fact, the idea of the welfare state assumes that money has a diminishing utility it doesn't benefit the rich as much as the poor, and thus the enforced government transfer of money from the rich to the poor is justified. But isn't it possible that individuals who work hard for their money deserve it, whether or not forcefully taking it maximizes utility? (For now, we omit questions about whether anyone can really deserve a lot more money than other people, as well as

Chapter 8 - Utilitarianism

questions about how legitimately one came into their money or whether taxation is really unjustified.)

This analysis also reveals another fundamental difficulty with utilitarianism. Everything is sacrificed to the net utility. But should all moral acts be judged by the consequences they produce?

7. The Problem with Consequences

The most important difficulty for utilitarianism is that it emphasizes consequences exclusively. Utilitarians claim that "the ends always justify the means," and therefore we can do anything to maximize utility as long as the consequences are good. For example, imagine that our neighbor opens our mail every day before we get home, and then meticulously closes and replaces it with such skill that we can't tell it has been opened. Furthermore, suppose the neighbor derives great satisfaction from this activity, and we never find out about it. When we are out of town and give him the key for emergencies, he rummages through our mail and personal effects, carefully replacing them before we return. He finds these activities immensely pleasurable, we never find out, and the net utility increases because his happiness increases. An act utilitarian would say the neighbor acts morally, but isn't there something wrong here? Should our privacy be sacrificed to the net utility?

Act utilitarians are willing to sacrifice privacy, rights, or even life itself to the net utility. Imagine a country sheriff who has been charged with finding the perpetrator of a recent homicide. The powerful elite of the town inform the sheriff that if he doesn't find the murderer, they will kill the inhabitants of the local Native American reservation since they believe a Native American committed the crime. The sheriff has no idea who committed the murder, but he does believe that framing some innocent individual will avert the ensuing riot which will almost certainly kill hundreds of innocent people. In other words, the sheriff maximizes utility by framing an innocent victim.

Now according to an act utilitarian, this analysis is certainly correct. Nonetheless, most individuals think something is terribly wrong with framing innocent persons. But why? If we don't frame the innocent victim, hundreds of people will die. True, something may foul our plan. For example, someone may find out that the victim has been framed. But this just repeats a critique of utilitarianism that we never know the consequences for certain. For the moment all the sheriff can do is the best he or she can. That is all anybody can do. And remember, if we don't frame the innocent victim, the blood of hundreds of other innocent victims is on our hands.

This is a situation in which a moral theory conflicts with our moral intuition. We *ordinarily* assume we shouldn't frame innocent people. But this is an *extraordinary* situation. Nevertheless, most of us think something is terribly wrong here. Maybe the theory can be reformulated to handle these cases?

8. The Problems with Rule Utilitarianism

Problems of this sort are precisely what led to the formulation of rule utilitarianism. Rule utilitarians claim that the rules "never violate a person's privacy," or "never frame innocent persons," maximize utility compared with the rules "sometimes violate a person's privacy," or "sometimes frame innocent persons." But rule utilitarianism is beset by its own unique difficulties.

A first problem is whether utilitarian rules allow exceptions. To illustrate, consider that the moral rule "never kill the innocent" maximizes utility compared to the rule "always kill the innocent," and thus a strict rule utilitarian adopts the former, from these two choices, without exceptions. But the rule "never kill the innocent

Chapter 8 - Utilitarianism

except to save more innocent lives" might maximize the utility better than either of the other two rules. If it did, a strict rule utilitarian would adopt it without exceptions. But this isn't the best possible rule either. The best possible rule is "never kill innocent people except when it maximizes the utility to do so." But if that is the best possible rule, *how is rule utilitarianism any different from act utilitarianism*?

The issue is further complicated by the fact that different interpretations of rule utilitarianism exist. In what we call *strong* rule utilitarianism, moral rules have no exceptions. In what we call *weak* rule utilitarianism, rules have some exceptions. The more exceptions we build into our moral rules, the weaker our version of rule utilitarianism becomes. But if we build enough exceptions into our moral rules, rule utilitarianism becomes indistinguishable from act utilitarianism.

Think about the traffic light again. A strict rule utilitarian says "don't go through traffic lights" because, compared with most other rules, this rule maximizes utility. If we compare it with the rules like "go through traffic lights when you want to," or "go through traffic lights if you're pretty sure you won't cause an accident," it fares well. But compare it with the rule: "don't go through traffic lights except in situations where it maximizes the utility to do so." A rule utilitarian should find this rule acceptable because it's the best conceivable rule. But if rule utilitarians act according to this rule, then their theory is indistinguishable from act utilitarianism.

Strong rule utilitarians can avoid this problem by not allowing exceptions to rules. They argue that if we make exceptions in individual cases, then the net utility will decrease because individuals naturally tend to be biased because they make exceptions that favor themselves. The act utilitarians counter by calling rule utilitarians superstitious "rule-worshipers." If it maximizes the utility to do "x," then why obey a rule that prescribes "y?" This issue could be resolved with some modified rule utilitarianism that would allow exceptions, but not collapse into the situational character of act utilitarianism. The attempt to formulate such rules completely has met with mixed success.

The second problem with rule utilitarianism is that it tells us to abide by the rules that maximize the utility if generally accepted. But suppose they aren't generally accepted? If we still abide by them we make useless sacrifices. Imagine that public television is conducting their annual fundraising campaign. A rule utilitarian reasons that if everyone abides by the rule, "give what you can to public television," the net utility will be increased. But suppose no one else contributes and public television goes broke? Then the individual that contributes has made a useless sacrifice. These objections show that many difficulties plague rule utilitarianism.

9. Conclusion

Let us conclude by comparing deontology and utilitarianism. Whereas deontology places moral value on something intrinsic to the agent, his/her intentions, utilitarianism places moral value on something extrinsic to the agent the action's consequences in terms of the happiness produced. For deontologists, the end never justifies the means; for utilitarians, the end always justifies the means. Note that both theories are based on a principle. For Kant, the principle is the categorical imperative and for Mill, it's the principle of utility. The ultimate principle of natural law is to promote the good or natural, and in contract theory, it's to do what is in our own interest. But maybe all of these theories are too formal and precise. Is there any theory of moral obligation that is less reliant on objective, abstract, moral principles, and more

Chapter 8 - Utilitarianism

contingent upon subjective, concrete, human experience? It's to such a theory that we now turn.

Chapter 9 – Existentialism

[Humans are] condemned to be free; because once thrown into the world, [they are] responsible for everything [they do.] ~ Jean-Paul Sartre

1. Basic Ideas of Existentialism

Could it be that all of the major ethical theories discussed so far are too precise and abstract to speak to an amorphous ethical reality? But perhaps precision in ethics is a chimera. The philosophers known as existentialists generally believed that all the major theories discuss thus far were mistaken—for precisely these reasons.

Existentialism is a philosophical movement whose origins are in the Danish philosopher Soren Kierkegaard (1813 – 1855) and the German philosopher Friedrich Nietzsche (1844 – 1900). Other major figures in the movement include, Karl Jaspers (1883 – 1969), Martin Heidegger (1899 – 1976), and Jean-Paul Sartre (1905 – 1980.) Existential philosophy is incredibly rich and diverse and its proponents include communists, socialists, atheists, theists, and nihilists. Despite this diversity, almost all existentialists share a few basic ideas that are relevant to our discussion.

Kierkegaard's rejection of a "rational and philosophical" Christianity serves as a starting point for our deliberation. He believed that Christianity erred by trying to be *reasonable*, when in fact it's based on faith and trust. Faith isn't a matter of affirming certain rational propositions, but of acting in a certain way. Kierkegaard made this point in his famous retelling of the biblical story of Abraham and his son Isaac. It wasn't reasonable for Abraham to sacrifice his son simply because God asked him to;

Chapter 9 – Existentialism

instead, following his God's orders was an act of faith. From an ethical point of view Abraham action was immoral, but for Kierkegaard faith and religion transcend reason and ethics.

These considerations lead to the *first* basic idea of existentialism: *reason is an inadequate instrument with which to comprehend the depth, mystery, and meaning of life.* Reason's limitations were poignantly described by the Russian novelist Feodor Dostoyevsky who said that while reason satisfies our rational selves, desire is the real manifestation of life. But as we saw in the first chapter, Western philosophy began when the Greeks used reason to understand the world. Greek rationalism led to a search for the rational and objective foundations of knowledge, meaning, truth, and value.

The existentialists reject this tradition. They repudiate the abstract, obtuse, specialized, esoteric, and formal subtlety which divorces the intellect from life. They maintain that life isn't an equation or riddle to be rationally resolved; it's more of a mystery to be lived. Reason can't resolve our most pressing existential concerns; it can't tell us the meaning of life. Theory, speculation, and metaphysical and moral abstraction are worth less than concrete reality. Thus *existentialism emphasizes concrete, personal experience over rational abstractions.* This is its *second* basic idea.

The emphasis on the concrete is also captured in the existential dictum "existence precedes essence." This means that we exist first, as particular, concrete, human subjects before we are defined by any universal, objective form or essence. Existence refers to 'that a thing is," while essence refers to "what a thing is." For instance, the essence of the four-legged, tail-wagging, car-chasing thing we often see is "dogness." That is what is! But the existentialist denies that there is any *human nature* that tells us what we are or what we ought to do; rather, we exist first as concrete human subjects and then proceed to create our essence. Fate or a God don't determine us, we determine ourselves. We may become saints or sinners, but it's up to us to decide. In the same way, moral theories can't tell us what to do. Intellectual theories are too detached from life to provide any guidance in our concrete lives. Theories may provide the rationale for human actions, but they can't command our assent.

We can easily see how moral theories can't make us do anything. The prescriptions of natural law, a social contract, the categorical imperative, or the net utility can't command our conduct because we can always ask, "Why follow these theories?" Moral theories may define our moral duties and obligations, but they mean nothing without *personal commitment*. Action "x" may violate the natural law, the social contract, the categorical imperative, and the greatest happiness principle but, "so what?" That doesn't tell us we shouldn't do "x." These theories assume ethics is objective, that some actions really are right or wrong. By contrast, existentialism emphasizes the human subject as the only ultimate source of morality. Only when we commit ourselves to some course of action do we act as moral agents.

The emphasis on personal commitment brings us to a *third* basic idea of existentialism: *human beings are radically free*. We are the ones who create the meaning, truth, and value in our lives, and we are totally responsible for our lives. We often claim to be unable to do certain things, but in fact, we don't do them because *we don't want to*. If we wanted to do them we would. For instance, the fact that it's wrong to steal doesn't prevent us from doing it, only we can do that. True, we can't do everything—we can't fly—but we can choose from our available options and, in the process, create our selves. In summary, existentialism claims that: Moral theories which derive from rational thinking are defective because *they emphasize personal abstraction over experience, and they can't*

Chapter 9 – Existentialism

account for the role that human freedom—manifested by personal commitment—plays in the moral domain.

2. Sartre And Freedom

The famous existentialist Jean-Paul Sartre (1905 – 1980) was a philosopher, playwright, political activist, and social critic. The complexities and nuances of his philosophy are formidable, but Sartre's philosophy best characterizes the unique features of an existential ethics. The key concepts in the Sartrean analysis of ethics are freedom, angst, bad faith, and authenticity. We discuss each in turn.

We begin our discussion with Sartre's notion that *we are radically free*. If we are in a bad mood, for example, it's because we choose to be. The external world doesn't impose itself upon our consciousness; we control our moods, thoughts, attitudes, and choices. And we aren't determined by our past choices! We can easily demonstrate.

Suppose we are trying to decide whether to study or drink beer. No theory or promise eliminates this choice. Early in the morning, we might say to ourselves, "tonight I will forego the beer and study." But when the evening comes we must make a choice, beer or books. Or suppose we promise ourselves that on Monday we will start a diet. But when Monday comes, our former promise means nothing. At that moment we must decide, diet or dessert? Our promises, ideas, and theories mean nothing because when the moment of choice arrives we stand face to face with human freedom. In the same way, our past promises don't determine our present choices, our present choices don't determine the future. No matter how we try to deny our freedom, it forces itself upon us.

For Sartre, freedom derives from human consciousness. We are conscious of both objects in the world and of ourselves as subjects, and this self-consciousness is the source of freedom. Self-conscious beings can imagine themselves as more muscular, attractive, knowledgeable, famous, or wealthy. In short, they can be conscious of what they lack, and can freely choose to fill these voids. Thus, freedom emanates from our consciousness of possibilities, particularly the possibility that we can be more than we are now. The concept of freedom is difficult to conceptualize and articulate precisely because Sartre says, it isn't an abstraction. Rather, it's intensely experienced in the moment of our actual, concrete choices.

Unfortunately, freedom is paradoxical. We are free to do anything except not make choices, thus *we cannot not be free*. We are, in Sartre's words, "condemned to be free." This frightening phrase captures the essence of the paradox of freedom. We can't escape freedom! To illustrate, suppose that we want to know if we should perform active euthanasia on our terminally ill parent. We can choose to do it or not, but we can't not choose because not choosing is itself a choice. There is no escape from the fact that human beings must choose and that they are thus responsible for their choices.

Consider another example. We are trying to choose between believing or disbelieving in the existence of the Judeo-Christian God. We can choose to believe, to not to believe or to hold our belief in abeyance. But any choice carries with it an awesome responsibility. If we believe because we think it's the safest choice or because we have been told to, we are responsible for our pragmatism or credulity. If we don't believe because we have no evidence or because we don't care, we are responsible for our skepticism or apathy. And if we don't choose at all, we are responsible for our indecision because not choosing is a choice itself. Thus we can't avoid making choices.

Chapter 9 – Existentialism

One way to try to escape our freedom is to accept creeds and theories which tell us what acts must be performed. But this doesn't solve the problem. We have simply taken the choice to another level where the question becomes, "what creeds should we subscribe to?" Thus there is no escape from the fact that we are prisoners of freedom. We are alone; we are without excuses. It seems we are "condemned to be free."

3. Angst, Bad Faith, and Authenticity

According to Sartre, when we encounter freedom and realize its paradox, we experience *angst* or anxiety. This anxiety results from the grave difficulty we have in accepting total responsibility for our acts. We are alone in the world without any guidance or any eternal principles to inform and console us. Instead, we must create our own values; we are like Gods! We experience the dread of knowing we can do *anything*. But angst, anxiety, or dread result from the complete responsibility that accompanies our freedom to create value.

So great is freedom and its accompanying angst, that it's easier to deny freedom by avoiding painful decisions and pretending that freedom doesn't exist. Sartre says there are three ways this can be done. The first is to fail to choose. But, as we have just seen, to not choose is itself a choice, thus non-choice doesn't allow one to escape from freedom. The second is to be what Sartre calls a "serious-minded" individual who pretends that some objective values dictate the right choice for them. But these values mean nothing unless we make them our own. They can't make us do anything.

Sartre's demonstrates how moral values fail in the example of the young man who must decide whether to stay home with his mother or go off to join the French Free forces fighting the Germans in

World War II. The young man's brother had been killed trying to stop the German offensive, and he wants to avenge his death, but his mother wants him to stay in France with her. What should he do?

Sartre claims that no moral theory could resolve this dilemma. It doesn't help to claim that the young man should do his duty since he experiences a conflict of duties. It doesn't help to recommend that he should do the good or the natural, inasmuch as he can't ascertain what the good or natural is. It's no help to follow the principle of utility either because he doesn't know what might happen. He might stay home and feel guilty, or go to war and be killed. He can't even be sure what is in his own interest. Sartre asserts that the young man must choose a course of action by himself and live with complete responsibility for the consequences. Abstract theories fail in real life situations, Sartre says, because real life isn't an esoteric puzzle. Life is about flesh and blood, men and women, and life and death.

The third and most important way to deny freedom is to act in *bad faith*. We act *inauthentically* or in bad faith by thinking of ourselves as passive objects manipulated by other people, social conventions, religious commands, or moral codes. In other words, *we deny our subjectivity*! Sartre tells the story of a young woman who is being slowly seduced. As the young man's hand begins to touch her, she pretends not to notice. She believes that something is happening *to her*, that she is a passive object. But she isn't. She is allowing this to happen and can stop the young man, and she acts in bad faith by pretending not to be free. Or consider students who don't want to read and study and who blame the teacher or school for their failure. They are mistaken; they could study hard. When we avoid painful decisions and pretend that we aren't free, we are acting in *bad faith*; we are refusing to take responsibility for our actions.

Chapter 9 – Existentialism

In perhaps his most famous example of bad faith, Sartre tells the story of a waiter who thinks of himself as an object controlled by the role he plays. He denies his freedom to leave at anytime, to just walk out. But Sartre says the waiter isn't controlled by the role, the rules, the society, moral theory, God, or anything else. He can be what he wants, even if that means becoming unemployed and living on the streets. It's the awesome nature of this responsibility that invites a retreat from freedom and exemplifies bad faith.

Our actions—not ethical theories or abstract principles—create our value. We often deny this and reduce our existential anxiety and doubt by accepting systems, theories, and principles that give certitude. But in so doing, we fail to ask questions and we don't actualize our potential to doubt and thereby be fully human. We refuse to search for the values that make life meaningful and don't confront with courage the anxiety that accompanies the creation of value in our own lives.

If we do have the courage to create value, the courage to commit to a course of action and accept full responsibility for our choices, we act *authentically*, or in good faith. Sartre doesn't say much about good faith except that it involves choosing the values, purposes, and projects for which we take full responsibility. Authentic individuals don't allow anything to dictate to them, they simply choose to *commit themselves* to a particular course of action.

4. Problems for an Existential Ethics

The most obvious problem for Sartre's ethics is whether freedom exists to the extent that he supposed, or if it exists at all. And there are other difficulties. Consider again the Sartrean project.

When acting in bad faith, we pretend that something controls our behavior. Now imagine individuals who live according to the moral principles with which they have been raised. Occasionally, they have considered that these principles may be groundless and that they could be rejected. However, the idea that they must create their own principles, values, and meaning in life is frightening. So they silence their doubts.

Sartre believes such individuals are morally culpable for accepting their initial moral principles, for supposing that these principles control them. But are such individuals really so bad? Suppose they are pleasant, dutiful, conscientious, and kind? Is it really true that those who deceive themselves into thinking they are controlled by moral rules, or who have never considered the possibility of other principles, are immoral? It doesn't seem so.

Now our appraisal would probably be different if these individuals had accepted were more dubious principles. If they had been taught since youth to torture animals and set houses on fire, we would likely condemn the actions that follow from their principles. But this suggests that we condemn their acts, not because they performed them in bad faith, but because their principles and actions are immoral. This suggests that it doesn't matter whether actions are done in good or bad faith, but whether the actions are good or bad.

The point becomes even clearer if we examine cases of actions done in good faith. Imagine individuals who strive all of their life to create their own values. After a long and arduous intellectual journey, they decide that there are no gods or objective values. Nonetheless, they dedicate their lives to working arduously in cancer research. They give no reason for their choice other than to say, "We freely commit ourselves to this project and take full responsibility for the outcome of our life." Whatever else we may think of it, there is something praiseworthy about this enterprise; this life lived in good faith.

Chapter 9 – Existentialism

This exemplifies what some existentialist call a project. Projects are self-created endeavors which allow us to experience freedom and authenticity. Whether our project is to be a parent, medical researcher, plumber, teacher, dancer, or concert pianist, the way we do it, according to Sartre, says more about the morality of the action than the action itself. This follows from the fact that there are no objective values. If we act in good faith—the unique expression of our own being with full recognition of our freedom and its attached responsibility—then we act morally.

The problem here is with sincere killers, torture advocates or Nazis. If they really believe they are doing the right thing—say killing for their gods—and they do it without hypocrisy and in good faith then, according to Sartre, they act morally. In fact, it doesn't matter what they do as long as it's done in good faith. Here we encounter the same problems that plagued other theories of subjective value. If there is no objective foundation to morality, then anything is allowable. Thus, good and bad faith are unable to distinguish between what we ordinarily assume are right and wrong actions. This suggests that something more is needed to understand the nature of morality than mere commitment. Is there any way for Sartre to avoid this conclusion?

5. Other Existential Thinkers

Sartre's could rely upon a God as the ultimate source of objective value, but Sartre was an atheist. For Kierkegaard, ethical principles have their place, but they are subservient to a God who can suspend them. Moreover, this God doesn't always share our moral judgments or the dictates of our moral conscience. If that were the case, we would only need our conscience in order to be moral, and would not need God. According to Kierkegaard, faith is higher than reason in the moral domain, inasmuch as moral principles and theological abstractions mean nothing without an intensely personal commitment to the moral or religious way of life.

Other religious existentialists have taken up the Kierkegaardian project. They generally reject proofs for the existence of a God and absolute moral principles. They emphasize human subjects and their freedom, accepting a God as the source of objective value. Thus a religious existential ethics rejects the rationalism of natural law ethics and, at least in Kierkegaard's case, moves in the direction of a divine command theory. However, by positing an objective source of morality, ethics may more properly be called religious than existential. Such theories are open to all the philosophical objections we may pose for any religious claim. A theological existentialism must be built upon a theology with all its attendant philosophical difficulties.

Another existentialist who tried to respond to the criticisms of existential ethics was the French writer Simone de Beauvoir (1908-1986). Like Sartre, de Beauvoir made freedom central to her ethics. In *The Ethics of Ambiguity*, she argued that we recognize the lack or the emptiness in our being and try to fill these spaces by freely choosing *projects*. We devote our labor to projects that, hopefully, disclose our unique being. By engaging in a project we experience the freedom to give our lives value and meaning. In the struggle to overcome the obstacles inherent in our project, we discover our own being as free.

De Beauvoir admits that ethics is ambiguous, but not that it's absurd. If life were absurd, nihilism follows. But amidst ambiguity, we have the opportunity to give life value and meaning. If values were transparent or translucent, we would not have this chance to disclose ourselves as free being through our projects. Since values are more opaque, the genuinely moral person lives in a world of

Chapter 9 – Existentialism

painful and continually questioning. Ambiguity provides the realm in which we may create our values.

In the final analysis, freedom was the ultimate value for de Beauvoir, and she opposed any action that limited human freedom. The ultimate precept is to respect the freedom of others. She gave the following example of how the precept worked. If others attempt suicide under the influence of intoxicants or temporary depression, we may interfere with their freedom. But if they want to end or ruin their lives after rational deliberation, we should allow them to do so.

Still, despite her claim to the contrary, it seems unlikely that freedom is the only value or even the most important one. For example, most people don't think that freedom is more important than justice or life itself. In addition, whenever principles other than freedom are introduced, we move away from the spirit of an existential ethics. This isn't to say that freedom can't function as the ultimate moral principle, only that if it does we have another objective moral theory.

6. An Assessment

If we really do create values by freely choosing projects, then there is no way to distinguish good projects or actions from bad ones, other than to say some are freely chosen and some aren't. But it just doesn't seem true that our commitment to something makes it valuable. Nor does it seem true that our lack of commitment makes something worthless. As with various elements of other theories we have examined, there is something counter-intuitive about existential ethics. It appears that the existential account of value is just too subjective.

Another difficulty with the existential theory of value is its irrationalism. If ethics is merely a matter of choosing, then no choice is irrational. If we ask existentialists why they chose "x," their only possible reply is, "we just choose." But this is unsatisfactory. If we can give no reason why we choose something, then our choice isn't rational. Existentialists can give no reason why they chose anything precisely because there is no reason to choose. If there were, then ethics would be rational and objective. This is another problem with the existential account of value; it's too irrational.

Of course, an existentialist rejects this critique. They argue that the whole point of an existential ethic is to show that reason is an inadequate instrument to understand morality. But are we really satisfied with a theory that can give us no reason why we ought to do something? If I tell you that you should go jump in the lake but can't tell you why, aren't you hesitant to do it? And doesn't this show that reason must play *some* role in ethics? Thus, even if the existentialists are right about reason's limitations, it doesn't follow that reason plays no role in the moral sphere.

Other existentialists try to overcome the subjectivism and irrationalism with God, freedom, or some other objective standard. But this undermines the radical nature of existentialism, suggesting that ethical theorizing is necessary to uncover the objective foundations of morality. Remember, existentialism was attractive because it proposed to bypass the task of uncovering the principles operative in the moral arena, but without principles existential ethics is bankrupt. The existentialists are correct when they argue that morality involves personal commitment, but if they can't tell us what o be committed to or why the theory is seriously deficient.

Chapter 10 – Evolution and Ethics

Man in his arrogance thinks himself worthy the interposition of a deity. More humble and I think truer to consider himself created from animals.
~ Charles Darwin

1. Darwin and Evolution

Charles Darwin (1809 -1882) was born into a wealthy and loving English family. His father was a physician who assumed his son would follow him into the profession but Darwin, squeamish at the site of blood, decided to study for the clergy at Cambridge. Darwin also had a great love for science and nature, and after graduation, he was offered a job as the naturalist aboard the H.M.S. Beagle, a ship that was to circumnavigate the globe. He was chosen because the captain, who couldn't socialize with his crew, found Darwin amicable company. So Darwin decided to delay his entry into the clergy and embark on a five-year journey that provided few comforts and for which he had to pay his own way. His journey would change the world.

When Darwin began his journey in 1831 almost everyone assumed that the world was: 1) about six thousand years old; 2) geologically stable; and 3) designed by an omnipotent creator. But the time was ripe to challenge all of these hypotheses. Evolution had been discussed for nearly a hundred years—including by Darwin's grandfather Erasmus Darwin—and the fossil evidence was already causing a stir, most notably due to the work of the geologist Sir Charles Lyell (1797 – 1875). In the course of his voyage, after observing and cataloging hundreds of species, a new idea slowly emerged in Darwin's mind. His insight was based on four basic facts, and two inferences from those facts. Here is a brief sketch of the conceptual skeleton of his theorizing in *The Origin of Species.*

The first two facts come from population ecology: 1) all species have great potential fertility; their populations will increase exponentially if all that are born survive; and 2) natural resources are limited. Indebted to Thomas Malthus' *An Essay on the Principle of Population,* Darwin realized that in nature there is a fierce struggle for existence since natural resources can't support all existent individuals. He then combined this logical inference with two facts from genetics: 1) individuals display variation; they aren't exactly alike; and 2) these variations are inherited. From these facts, Darwin inferred that, in the struggle for existence, some individuals will live longer, reproduce and pass their hereditary constitution on to future generations. This process is called *natural selection*. Thus: variation + inheritance + struggle for existence + natural selection = extinction or gradual change of species.

To better understand natural selection, consider *artificial selection*, which Darwin himself used to help explain his ideas. Almost everyone knows you breed specific types of animals to produce certain kinds of offspring. If you want a big dog, you mate big dogs, if you want a fast horse, you mate fast horses. Darwin knew that variations are inherited, but no one in the nineteenth-century understood the process by which hereditary information was transmitted. That would have to wait for Gregor Mendel and the science of genetics.

The modern theory of evolution resulted from one the greatest scientific achievements in human history, the Neo-Darwinian or modern synthesis of the 1930s and 1940s. It combined Darwinian natural selection with Mendelian genetics to form a more powerful theory. This theory was further solidified in 1952 with the

Chapter 10 – Evolution and Ethics

discovery of DNA by Crick and Watson which led to an understanding of evolution at the molecular level.

Today, biological evolution is confirmed every single day in laboratories around the world, over and over again. Biological evolution, the idea that we share a common ancestry with all life, is now supported by a broad spectrum of sciences including, but not limited to: embryology, molecular biology, geology, chemistry, genetics, population ecology, ecology, zoology, botany, comparative anatomy, fossil evidence, and more. Evolutionary theory has the same scientific status as gravitational, atomic, quantum, or relativity theories. Simply stated, *biological evolution is true beyond any reasonable doubt. Anyone who tells you otherwise is either scientifically illiterate or lying to you.*

2. Evolution and Ethics

But how is evolution relevant for ethics? First, any understanding of human nature—crucial for understanding ethics—must take into account our evolutionary heritage. In fact, ethical theories often differ because they use different theories of human nature. Moral theories claim that human nature is basically good, bad, self-interested, rational, sympathetic, radically free, and so on. Surely then *the* scientific theory of human nature is relevant to ethics.

To understand how evolution applies in various domains consider that Darwin originally proposed a theory about the evolution of plant and non-human animal bodies. Subsequently, in *The Descent of Man*, he extended the argument to human bodies. Today we have extended evolutionary ideas further—to minds and behaviors. Evolutionary epistemology examines the nature and limits of minds over time and the evolution of ideas and concepts in the history of science and in the developing child. That minds like bodies evolve over time is the fundamental starting point of evolutionary epistemology.

Evolutionary psychologists extend evolutionary ideas to human behavior. We now understand human behaviors like courtship, mating, aggression, and religion in a biological context. Evolutionary ethicists begin with the fact of evolution and proceed to explore the connection between biology and ethical behaviors. They ask questions like: Can we derive moral obligations from evolutionary facts? Does ordinary morality oppose or complement evolution? How were moral behaviors selected for? Do non-human animals exhibit rudimentary moral behaviors? Do moral behaviors evolve? Do moral concepts evolve? Can we reconcile a survival instinct with moral prescriptions? In short, evolutionary ethicists want to know how evolution sheds light on morality.

3. Social Darwinism

One of the first philosophers to take note of Darwin's ideas was his contemporary Herbert Spencer (1820 – 1903), the man who coined the phrase, "survival of the fittest." Spencer believed that the struggle for existence entailed both competition and cooperation; he meant to reconcile biology and morality. But many went further, including the American capitalists Rockefeller and Carnegie, believing that Spencer's interpretation of Darwin justified cut-throat economic competition. They believed that the idea of the survival of the fittest justified the domination of the rich over everyone else; it justified their wealth and power.

Social Darwinism, the idea that individuals and groups are subject to natural selection, was thus born. It would be used to justify imperialism, conservatism, and racism. Social Darwinism found its most eloquent spokesperson in the Yale sociologist William Graham Sumner (1840 – 1910). He agreed with the

Chapter 10 – Evolution and Ethics

greedy capitalists that we should allow the struggle for existence to proceed without intervention. In the ensuing struggle, the strong will succeed and the weak will fail. This is as it should be.

There are a number of problems with this approach. In the first place, there isn't anything necessarily better or biologically fitter about rich individuals. Many have a lot of money because they were born into wealth, had certain talents that happened to benefit them in a certain kind of economy, or just got lucky. (As the American billionaire Warren Buffet says, in many environments, he would have been one of the weak ones.) Moreover, the whole idea conflicts with our moral intuition. Amassing huge fortunes while enslaving or exterminating others isn't most people's idea of moral behavior. And, as we will see, the desire to dominate others is only part of our evolutionary heritage.

4. Evolution and Ethics Opposed

About this time another one of Darwin's great defenders argued that ethics and evolution were radically incompatible. Thomas Henry Huxley (1825–1895) was a member of one of the most famous families in England and an ardent supporter of Darwin. He defended Darwinism in a series of lectures and debates, of which the most famous was his encounter with Bishop Samuel Wilberforce (1805–1873), the most renowned cleric in England at that time. During the debate, Wilberforce sarcastically inquired into whether Huxley was descendent from monkeys on his father or mother's side. Huxley is purported to have replied: "I would rather be the offspring of two apes than a man afraid to face the truth." A woman in attendance is said to have fainted.

Years later in 1893 at Oxford, Huxley delivered the Romanes lectures, at the time the most important philosophical lectures in the world. There Huxley compared the *state of nature* or natural

Philosophical Ethics: Theory And Practice

processes—nature before human intervention—with *the state of art* or artificial processes—nature altered by human intervention. These two states are in a kind of natural antagonism. Huxley used a metaphor to make his point. Imagine a piece of land in its natural state that is subsequently transformed by someone into a garden. If this gardener stops cultivating the garden, it will return to its natural state. This image illustrates the natural antagonism between the human created state of art and the state of nature.

Huxley proceeded to argue that while it's true that humans are part of nature, this doesn't show that nature and art are compatible. A virus is a part of us, but antagonistic toward us. Huxley thought that natural processes always conflict with artificial ones, a point he reinforced with another metaphor. In the same way, we create a garden by combating nature, we bring about an ideal society by combating our natural tendencies. An ideal society values cooperation, sympathy, and self-restraint; the state of nature values competition, ruthlessness, and self-interest. Thus ethics demands that we oppose, not acquiesce, to nature. As Huxley put it: "Let us understand, once and for all, that the ethical progress of society depends, not on imitating the cosmic process, still less in runny away from it, but in combating it." (Katherine Hepburn made the same point to Humphrey Bogart in the film, The African Queen, when she said: "Nature, Mr. Allnut, is what we are put in this world to rise above.")

Huxley believed that ethical progress manifests itself in cultural evolution—the evolution of science, art, religion, politics and other elements of culture. But he also believed that powerful natural forces, operating both within and outside of us, eventually overwhelm all artificial processes, all human cultural creations. Human will continue to oppose nature by creating and developing civilizations "until the evolution of our globe shall have entered so far upon its downward course that the cosmic process resumes its

Chapter 10 – Evolution and Ethics

sway; and, once more, the state of nature prevails over the surface of our planet." It seems, in the end, we are doomed; nature will reclaim all that it has lost; evolution has little to offer ethics.

5. Evolution and Ethics Conjoined

In 1943, exactly fifty years after his grandfather had delivered the Romanes lecture, Julian Huxley (1887 – 1975) gave the address. J. Huxley, one of the world's greatest biologists at the time, argued that ethics and evolution were compatible. To illuminate the idea, Huxley looked at the history of cosmic evolution. Inorganic evolution was painstakingly slow, but after eons of time led to biological evolution. This, in turn, led to conscious human beings who in turn brought about a psycho-social evolution. Now education, tradition, and language expedite the evolutionary process, and conscious beings now create ethical imperatives and goals for the species. (Thus ought comes from is.)

The two basic goals of the evolutionary process should be individual development and social cohesion. The goal, or the meaning of life if you will, is the full development of human potential. Huxley also believed evolution was orthogenetic—progressing toward the emergence of new and better forms of being. Ethical behaviors promote this progressive march of evolution toward achieving our goals. This isn't surprising because in nature there is an unconscious striving toward ends or goals. As Huxley put it: "… [humans] impose moral principles upon ever-widening areas of the cosmic process, in whose further slow unfolding [they are] now the protagonist. [They] can inject [their] ethics into the heart of evolution." It seems that evolution is the key to understanding both ethical imperatives and, ultimately, the meaning of our lives.

We might also mention the French Jesuit Pierre Teilhard de Chardin (1881 – 1955), who developed an evolutionary Christianity which parallels some of J. Huxley's ideas. Teilhard understood evolution to be an orthogenesis moving toward an omega or endpoint. According to Teilhard, God made matter which in turn created consciousness, and all three will be reunited at the omega point which is a society of hyper-persons in unity with God. Ethical imperatives are those which promote the realization of the omega point. Thus for both J. Huxley and Teilhard evolution is the key to understand what we ought to do which is, roughly, play our role in bringing about higher levels of being and consciousness.

6. Ethics and Sociobiology

In the mid-1970s a new science emerged which studies the evolutionary aspects of animal and human social behaviors. And that science, *sociobiology*, defends an evolutionary ethics by reducing ethical behaviors to biological ones. The preeminent spokesperson and the founding father of sociobiology is the Harvard biologist E. O. Wilson (1929 –).

Wilson agrees with Julian Huxley that ethics arises from the evolutionary process, but disagrees that evolution is directed or consciously moving toward some goal. In fact, the great human dilemma is that evolution has no goal, end or purpose. To illustrate, consider that the protective coloring of certain moths doesn't happen *in order for* them to survive, nor does it happen *because* there is a threat from predators. Instead, there are simply random genetic mutations which are then subject to environmental selection. The fact that some moths or homo sapiens survive is an evolutionary accident. There isn't anything within organisms that directs them to some end.

Chapter 10 – Evolution and Ethics

To understand ethics without teleology we must show that there is some advantage to ethical behavior; we must show ethical-type behaviors aid survival. The first clue to understanding this came from research showing that the beneficiaries of altruistic behavior in non-human animals were generally individuals who shared many genes with the altruist. While the altruist's behavior lowered his or her chance of survival, it increased the survival of kin. This biological favoring of genetic relatives is called *kin selection*. It is why we are more willing to die for our own children than for other people's children.

In addition, there is a more general altruism observed in both human and non-human animals that goes beyond close genetic relatives. This is called *reciprocal altruism* because it relies on reciprocity. The biological evidence for it derives from the pioneering work of Robert Trivers who noted warning cries in birds and cleaning symbiosis as classic examples. Natural selection sometimes favors cooperative behaviors that increase chances for a species survival; self-interest is often served better by cooperation than competition. Thus, ethical behaviors can be selected for.

Wilson also draws a distinction between hard-core and soft-core altruism. *Hard-core altruism* hasn't anything to do with reciprocity and is usually directed toward our closest kin. *Soft-core altruism* depends on reciprocity and is ultimately selfish. Wilson, one of the world's foremost experts on social insects, has observed that their behavior is mostly hard-core, while human beings carry soft-core altruism to extremes. We specialize in reciprocity between non-biologically related individuals.

Furthermore, Wilson argues that all elaborate forms of social organization find their basis in individual welfare. Contracts and other agreements are the kind of soft-core altruism that makes human social interaction possible. The genius of human civilizations the ease with which we make and break these soft-core relationships. But this is a good thing. If altruism were all hard-core we would continually engage in tribal warfare, and the social rules that serve our self-interest would be impossible to maintain. Buried deep within our brains is the knowledge that soft-core (reciprocal) altruism aids our survival. Moral consciousness emanates from these deep reservoirs.

Recently E. O. Wilson and the philosopher of science Michael Ruse have advanced a new theory of morality. They reject any theory that asserts that nature evinces values as evolutionary change unfolds because that reads values into evolution. So they reject theories like Julian Huxley's because it has no biological foundation. Instead, Wilson and Ruse forge a connection between ethics and evolution without committing the naturalistic fallacy. They begin with two scientific premises: 1) social behavior of animals is under the control of genes; and 2) humans are animals. Since both premises are true, we are led to a distinctively biological human morality based on kin selection.

Now how did nature make us moral? The clue is our intelligence. We are hard-wired for a number of instinctive behaviors—aversion to insects, fear of snakes and heights, etc. Altruism is also hard-wired since it has adaptive advantages. But how do we understand this with our conscious minds? We consciously understand the biological imperatives underneath morality as objective moral codes. Nature makes us believe in moral codes; biology is the foundation of morality.

What Wilson and Ruse are saying is that the human species has evolved both hard-core and soft-core altruistic tendencies. Evolution and ethics are compatible. However there are no absolute foundations for ethics, moral beliefs simply serve our reproductive aims and help us survive. *Ethics is essentially an*

Chapter 10 – Evolution and Ethics

illusion our genes use to get us to cooperate. If we had a different evolutionary history our ethics would be very different.

Yet this doesn't lead to moral relativism; which ethical behaviors we adopt matter in terms of our survival. Even without objective foundations, we face social problems that overwhelm biology, so understanding biology is just the first step in solving our problems. Morality is a legacy of evolution, not a reflection of divine verities.

7. Critics of Sociobiology

The late paleontologist Stephen Jay Gould (1941 – 2002) argued that sociobiology confuses supposable notions of biological potential with the more doubtful notion of biological determinism. It is one thing to say that our genes determine the range of our behaviors and social institutions, but quite another to say that our genes determine social institutions.

Gould, an ardent defender of Darwinism, rejects Wilson's generalization of the causes of behavior in lower animals to such causes human beings. While human behavior is clearly biologically based and adaptive, humans have gone far beyond other species in developing a non-biological means to transmit adaptive behavior to future generations. This means that human social behaviors like morality and religion have evolved far from the reach of genetic control. Thus human culture, rather than genetic controls, determines virtually all of our social behaviors.

Gould does admit that reciprocal altruism exists, but this doesn't necessitate a genetic coding corresponding to the behavior. Even though the range of our potential is limited by biology, Gould doubts that there is a genetic base to most social behaviors which excludes the role cultural evolution plays in directing human actions. What evidence is there that genes control specific social behavior? Gould says there is none, and even if there were our large brain can potentially overcome biological determinism.

Another recent critique of sociobiology is the scientist and philosopher Francisco J. Ayala (1934 -), who has advanced a number of powerful arguments to sever the connection that sociobiologists make between moral norms and natural selection. First, inasmuch as moral norms differ between cultures and across time without a corresponding difference in biology, the theory that morality depends upon biology is flawed. This evidence suggests that culture, not biology, plays the largest role in shaping behavior. Second, human intellectual abilities have the power to go beyond biology. For instance, we may be biologically territorial, but we can decide to forego this instinct.

Ayala also distinguishes between two senses of altruism. We define *biological altruism* in terms of the genetic consequences of a certain behavior. Genes may prompt these behaviors even though the fitness of the individual is diminished, but such behaviors haven't anything to do with ethical norms. They aren't ethical behaviors. On the other hand, *moral altruism* concerns intentions and motivations, with the regard we have for others; they have nothing to do with biology. Behaviors may look similar from the outside, but we distinguish them by the moral agent's conscious intentions. So Ayala affirms that reciprocal altruism in non-human animals isn't moral behavior anymore than we would describe social insects which die for their community as morally heroic.

In trying to explain the connection between ethics and evolution, Ayala differentiates between whether: 1) biology determines the "capacity" for ethics and whether 2) biology determines "particular" ethical norms or principles. He answers yes to the first question, but no to the latter. We are necessarily ethical, but particular norms themselves are freely chosen. The capacity for

Chapter 10 – Evolution and Ethics

ethics is intertwined with self-consciousness, a product of biological evolution, but the norms and principles of ethics are products of cultural, not biological, evolution. Thus he agrees with Gould that biology shapes our potential moral behaviors, but doesn't determine them.

Biology determines this *capacity* for ethics because of the presence in human beings of three necessary and sufficient conditions for ethical behavior which themselves derive from human consciousness. First, we anticipate the consequences of our actions because we can create mental images of unreal or imaginary possibilities. Second, we make value judgments about actions, ends, objects, and behaviors which we consider valuable. Third, we choose between courses of action. Ayala doesn't believe that evolution favored certain ethical behaviors, but that it did provide the conditions under which human consciousness, the source of all ethics, developed.

Turning to the question of whether evolution determines "particular" moral norms, Ayala claims that any attempt to justify particular moral norms with biology commits the naturalistic fallacy. Simply because evolution has proceeded in a particular way says nothing about whether it's right or good. The fact that bacteria have survived for millions of years doesn't mean they are more or less valuable than vertebrates. Instead, moral codes come from religious and social traditions. Thus, while morality must take into account biological knowledge, it's insufficient for deciding which moral codes should be accepted.

8. Problems for Evolutionary Ethics

It's difficult to advance a specific critique of evolutionary ethics because evolutionary ethics is a generic name for a number of interrelated, but nevertheless oftentimes contradictory theories.

However, there is one general criticism of the attempt to derive moral values from facts of nature that we have previously discussed—the naturalistic fallacy. The idea is that we can't derive values from facts, or ought from is. In this case, it means that just because of ethical behaviors arise in nature doesn't mean we should value those behaviors.

In addition, there is another problem sometimes referred to as the genetic fallacy. We commit this fallacy when we confuse the origin of a belief or behavior with its justification. Our belief in witches may have originated in our religious upbringing, but that doesn't mean we are justified in the belief. Analogously, soft-core altruism may have arisen because it bestowed evolutionary advantage, but that doesn't mean it's ethically justified. It's easy to confuse the genesis of an idea or behavior with its justification.

Thus, the critics argue, an adequate ethical theory must explain not only what we do and why, but what we *should* do. In other words, we must not only explain the nature and genesis of morality, we must justify it. But evolutionary ethicians have a hard time doing this. If they explain the genesis by saying that facts justify values, they commit the naturalistic fallacy. If they say that facts elicit values in an upward ethical progress, they mistakenly read purposes and ends into evolution that evolutionists assure us aren't there. In short, it may be that evolution explains the origin of morality, but it can't justify morality. Or it may be that these objections aren't valid, as other contemporary thinkers maintain.

Chapter 11 – Abortion

...research on human reproduction shows that the 'moment of conception' isn't a moment at all. Sometimes several sperm penetrate the outer membrane of the egg and it takes time for the egg to eject the extra chromosomes ... but even when a single sperm enters, its genes remain separate from those of the egg for a day or more, and it takes yet another day or so for the newly merged genome to control the cell. So the 'moment of conception' is in fact a span of twenty-four to forty-eight hours." ~ Steven Pinker

1. Biological Humans Are People

A fundamental question is: How do you determine humanity? In Christian theology, this is the question of ensoulment. In "An Almost Absolute Value in History," the Catholic philosopher and judge John T. Noonan (N) doesn't defend ensoulment. Instead, he argues: "If you are conceived by human parents you are human." He also quickly attacks other criteria of humanity like:

Viability – the idea that one becomes human when one can live without and isn't absolutely dependent upon, the mother. N counters: 1) viability depends on the current state of technology hence isn't a good guide; and 2) even when viable, fetuses and young children are dependent suggesting that the lessening of dependence doesn't confer humanity.

Experience – humanity depends on the formation of experience and memories. N counters: 1) fetuses have experiences from about 8 weeks; 2) even if all memories and experience is lost, say in total amnesia, humanity isn't lost; and 3) it isn't clear why experiences make one human since many humans fail to have important experiences.

Less sentiment – We suffer more grief at the loss of a child compared to a fetus. N counters: 1) feelings toward others isn't a good guide to their humanity; and 2) the ability to sense a thing isn't a good guide to its humanity.

Social visibility – fetuses don't communicate with other persons so they aren't members of society. N counters: 1) humanity doesn't depend on social recognition and when it does grave consequences follow for human beings.

N acknowledges that many philosophers hold that humanity isn't an objective concept. N argues that morality demands we assume an objective sense of humanity in order to answer moral questions. [This is hugely debatable; moreover, objective conceptions of humanity have led to monstrous results.]

Now N considers the following. The chance of a sperm becoming a person is about 1 in 200,000,000; the chance of eggs becoming human nearly 1,000,000 to 1. But the chance of a fertile egg becoming human is about 80%. (The actual probability is much less since between 2/3 & 3/4 of the fertilized eggs never attach to the uterine wall. So it seems that nature, or god if you will, is a great abortionist.) This dramatic change in probabilities doesn't definitively establish humanity but does suggest a non-arbitrary point at which we might assume it. We would hold you responsible for shooting something that was probably a human, but not for shooting something that was almost certainly not human. What this argument shows is that conception is the most plausible marker of humanity. Destroying a sperm is a lot different than destroying a fetus. In addition, after conception, there is a human genetic code.

Still, none of this means that abortion is never justified, only that the rights of the fetus are important and need to be balanced with other's rights. So abortion is justified to save the life of the mother since this is a case of self-defense.

Chapter 11 – Abortion

Reflection – It seems that N has explained what makes something human, a human genome, but not what makes it a person, which is something entirely different.

2. Abortion Is Immoral

Don Marquis' 1989 article, "Why Abortion Is Immoral" is the most celebrated pro-life piece in the literature. Marquis (M) begins by noting that few philosophers think abortion is immoral; in fact, the pro-life position has almost no contemporary philosophical support:

> The view that abortion is, with rare exceptions, seriously immoral has received little support in the recent philosophical literature. No doubt most philosophers affiliated with secular institutions of higher education believe that the anti-abortion position is either a symptom of irrational religious dogma or a conclusion generated by seriously confused philosophical argument. The purpose of this essay is to undermine this general belief.

He assumes, but doesn't try to prove, "that whether or not abortion is morally permissible stands or falls on whether or not a fetus is the sort of being whose life it's seriously wrong to end." M then asks: "why is killing an adult wrong." Killing is wrong, he says, because of its effect on the victim—specifically because it takes away a person's future. This explains why: 1) killing is so bad; and 2) why premature death is particularly bad.

This view gains additional support because: 1) it shows why it would be wrong to kill other intelligent extraterrestrials; 2) it shows why it would be wrong to kill some non-human animals; 3) it doesn't rule out active euthanasia; and 4) it easily accounts for the wrongfulness of young children (something personhood theories have trouble with).

Since eliminating an adult's future is what makes killing it wrong, abortion is wrong prima facie (at first glance.) And this doesn't rely on the fetus being a person. [According to this view, it would seem that killing a fetus is more wrong than killing a child, which is more wrong than killing an adult, etc.]

To better explain the structure of his argument he draws an analogy with an argument against animal cruelty. In both cases, the wrongness is explained by the appeal to a natural property—pain and suffering or denial of a future—without resorting to personhood. None of this shows that abortion is always wrong, just that it usually is.

And contraception isn't immoral on this view. Neither sperm nor ovum can possibly be considered a person and contraception can't be considered to deny all possible sperm and egg combinations which are possible since there are so many possible futures at the time contraception is used. (This might imply that contraception is worse since it denies millions of possible futures. Also, at what point are we denying this future then? After the 24-48 hours of conception I would assume.)

Conclusion – Since a fetus has a future, which is what makes killing wrong, killing a fetus is wrong. This resolves the standard problem of abortion which is to determine some property that makes a fetus more like a person than a group of cells—brain waves, viability, etc. That property is its possible future.

Reflections – Remember, even if you think abortion is morally wrong, that doesn't imply that you have a right to use the coercive power of the law to prevent others ending their pregnancies. To endorse that would entail a justification of the use of legal coercion on the ground that you are preventing harm to others (fetuses). The

Chapter 11 – Abortion

problem is that not all share the view that fetuses are persons. (In fact, granting fetuses full moral rights is a radical view that virtually no moral philosophers endorse—as Marquis admitted at the beginning of his essay.) If people disagree about whether something is a person, then what do you do if you can't convince them of your view? Kill them? Petition the government to coerce them? Try to convince them rationally but if unsuccessful let them alone?

3. A Defense of Abortion

Judith Jarvis Thomson's (T) imaginative examples and controversial conclusions have made "A Defense of Abortion" perhaps "the most widely reprinted essay in all of contemporary philosophy."

T doesn't think the conceptus is a person from the moment of conception, anymore than an acorn is an oak tree. But, for the sake of argument, she will grant this claim and ask if the permissibility of abortion follows. Assuming the personhood of the fetus, the anti-abortionist argument proceeds thus:

> Every person has a right to life. So the fetus has a right to life. No doubt the mother has a right to decide what shall happens in and to her body; everyone would grant that. But surely a person's right to life is stronger and more stringent than the mother's right to decide what happens in and to her body, and so outweighs it. So the fetus may not be killed; an abortion may not be performed.

T responds with a thought experiment:

> You wake up in the morning and find yourself back to back in bed with an unconscious violinist. A famous unconscious violinist. He has been found to have a fatal

kidney ailment, and the Society of Music Lovers has canvassed all the available medical records and found that you alone have the right blood type to help. They have therefore kidnapped you, and last night the violinist's circulatory system was plugged into yours, so that your kidneys can be used to extract poisons from his blood as well as your own ... [If he is unplugged from you now, he will die; but] in nine months he will have recovered from his ailment, and can safely be unplugged from you.

While it would be kind of you to let the violinist stay attached to your body, almost no one would think you are morally obligated to do so. This suggests that abortion is morally permissible in cases of rape. Of course, strong opponents of abortion may still say that one has a right to life even if one is conceived as a result of rape or the mother's life is in danger. (T calls the latter "the extreme view.")

Section 1 – How are we to defend the anti-abortion position in cases where the mother will die if she brings the child to full term? We could say that abortion kills the innocent child, whereas the mother will merely be allowed to die. But T argues that cases of self-defense are clearly not murder.

The abortion debate often focuses on what a 3rd party (a dr. for example) may do when a woman asks for an abortion (since it's very difficult to do this herself.) Now a 3rd party may say they don't want to kill a growing child trapped with you in a tiny house. But surely you have the right of self-defense in that situation. This shows the extreme view of abortion is false.

Section 2 – The anti-abortionist (AA) could change their argument and say abortion is ok in cases of self-defense but 3rd parties can't perform them, only pregnant women can. But this is false. If you own the house that the growing child is expanding in

Chapter 11 – Abortion

you have more right to it than he/she does. Thus, 3rd parties should recognize this just as they would recognize the one who owns the coat has a right to it. One can say that they don't want to get the coat back or perform the abortion, but they shouldn't say that someone else shouldn't do this—kill a person who is threatening another's life. Since abortion in cases of self-defense has been defended, T turns to other possibilities.

Section 3 – Does having the right to life mean I have a right to the bare minimum that it takes to keep me alive? Suppose that the only thing that will keep me alive is if Nicole Kidman flies from CA and kisses me or gives me one of her kidneys. Does this mean she has to share her kidney with me? No. Nobody has a right to her kidneys unless she gives them that right. It might be nice of her to do this, but I don't have the right to demand she does it. Now suppose that the right to life means I have the right not to be killed. Even so, my right to life doesn't give me the right to use your body (unless you give me permission.) So even if my life isn't threatened by your using my kidneys for 9 months, I don't have to give you permission to do so.

Section 4 – "In the most ordinary sort of case, to deprive someone of what he has a right to is to treat him unjustly … [but] The right to life consists not in the right not to be killed, but rather in the right not to be killed unjustly." You don't kill something unjustly if you kill it so you don't have to share your kidneys with it. So the argument against abortion must show it's unjust killing. In the case of rape, no permission is granted and thus the killing of the fetus is justified.

But what about the cases of voluntary sexual activity? In those cases, did the woman invite the fetus in and does the fetus now have a right to the woman's body? And how do we determine the extent of this responsibility? If a woman opens her window or leaves her house knowing there are rapists in the world (or just charming men) is she then responsible if she gets pregnant? Or suppose she installs bars on her windows (contraception) and burglars (or charming men) get in anyway even though she took precautions. Is she responsible and does the fetus now have a right to her body? Or suppose:

> Peopleseeds drift about in the air like pollen, and if you open your windows, one may drift in and take root in your carpets or upholstery. You don't want children, so you fix up your windows with fine mesh screens, the very best you can buy. As can happen, however, and on very, very rare occasions does happen, one of the screens is defective; and a seed drifts in and takes root. Does the personplant who now develops have a right to the use of your house?

We can hardly expect you never go outside or have a hysterectomy or only travel with an army. We would have to figure out all these cases but in some cases, abortion would be unjust killing and some not. [We could have a continuum from you never leave home to you sell yourself on the street to get pregnant so you can have an abortion. The point is that every case is different. So as your responsibility for becoming pregnant increases, so to do does your obligation to carry to full term. But your responsibility isn't the only factor to consider. We must also consider how much you are inconvenienced.]

Section 5 – You were kidnapped by the violinist (raped) but he only needed one hour at no risk to your health. In such cases, you ought not to abort. But this doesn't mean the violinist has a right to use your kidney. [Of course, if you became pregnant in the usual way, this would be even clearer.] It may be nice to share my chocolates, but you don't have a right to them if they're mine. Even if Angela Jolie is right across the room and only needs to kiss

Chapter 11 – Abortion

me to save my life, I have no right to her kiss, even though it would not be nice of her to refuse. So even if only an hour of the mother's body is needed to save a life—the mother isn't morally required to do so. [Does it follow that if I invited the fetus in and then want to kick them out and it won't go, that I have a right to kill it?]

Section 6 – "We have in fact to distinguish between the two kinds of Samaritan: the Good Samaritan and what we might call the Minimally Decent Samaritan." The law doesn't require we be even MDC but "in most states in this country women are compelled by law to be not merely Minimally Decent Samaritans, but Good Samaritans to unborn persons inside them." To be consistent, anti-abortionists should work for GS laws.

And if you ask us to keep you from being a GS or a very GS, (not remain pregnant) we should probably help you if you don't want to be in bed with the violinist for 9 months or years.

Section 7 – Even if the fetus is a person the impermissibility of abortion doesn't follow. But maybe it's that the fetus "is a person for whom the woman has a special kind of responsibility issuing from the fact that she is its mother" that makes abortion immoral. Here we must distinguish between cases in which parents didn't try to avoid pregnancy, take children home with them, etc. and thus are responsible from cases in which they tried not to conceive, etc. In some cases, abortion would be justified. [Again, each case is different.]

Section 8 – However if pregnancy only requires being a MDS, then one shouldn't abort. In other cases, one should abort. [Who should decide this, mother, parents, churches, states, etc.?]But the mother has no right to insist on the death of the fetus if it somehow can survive.

T concludes by noting she has assumed the fetus is a person, but early abortions clearly don't kill persons. [Her acorn, oak tree argument.]

4. Fetuses Aren't People

Mary Anne Warren's 1973 piece, "On the Moral and Legal Status of Abortion," is considered a classic of the literature and still reprinted in college textbooks. She tries to show that the fetus isn't a person, and hence not worthy of full moral rights. Most anti-abortion arguments don't do this, but instead defend abortion by: 1) pointing out the negative consequences of restricting access; or 2) claim the woman controls her body. But both arguments are problematic.

The key question for Warren is whether the fetus is a person. She begins by admitting that Judith Jarvis Thomson had a key insight—even if a fetus has rights, that doesn't mean they supersede a woman's.

Section 1 – She argues that we can't conclusively demonstrate that abortion is permissible if the fetus has a right to life. Thomson's argument fails in that the anti-abortionist may argue that one is responsible for the child except in rape cases. If we change the violinist story, it appears we may still be obligated to save the violinist. Thus we must deal with the ontological status of the fetus.

Section 2 – The question is: "How are we to define the moral community, the set of beings with full and equal moral rights, such that we can decide whether a human fetus is a member of this community or not?" Two questions arise: 1) what is a human (genetic sense of human) and more importantly 2) what is a person (moral sense of human)?

Chapter 11 – Abortion

To be a person you must satisfy at least 2 or 3 of her criteria for personhood which are:

1. Consciousness (of objects and events external and/or internal to the being), and in particular the capacity to feel pain;
2. Reasoning (the developed capacity to solve new and relatively complex problems);
3. Self-motivated activity (an activity which is relatively independent of genetic or direct external control).
4. The capacity to communicate, messages of with an indefinite number of possible contents on indefinitely many possible topics.
5. The presence of self-concepts and self-awareness.

The problem is that fetuses satisfy none of these criteria. Thus a fetus isn't a person by any objective measure and therefore not a member of the moral community.

This raises 2 other questions: 1) how like a human does something have to be to have a right to life and 2) do potential people have a right to life? Regarding 1, a fetus isn't very person like, in fact, less so than a mature fish (according to her criteria). Regarding 2, the rights of potential people, even millions of them can't outweigh the rights of actual people. Even if they could kill you and make millions of people out of you, you still have the right to escape (self-defense). Or even if you only had to be captured for nine months or a day (pregnancy) or even if you had been captured because of carelessness (you were partly responsible, never completely responsible as the man has some responsibility) you still have a right to escape no matter how many potential people might be born because the rights of an actual person always outweigh the rights of potential persons.

The argument doesn't apply to infanticide, W notes, because while in her body the woman has the primary say as to what happens to the fetus, whereas after something is born, she no longer does.

5. Christianity and Abortion

While it's true that most professional philosophers don't find abortion morally problematic, many Christian theologians do oppose abortion. And many Christians think they must oppose abortion on religious grounds. But must they? Does Church authority or Christian scripture unequivocally oppose abortion? The answer to these questions isn't clear.

First, it's generally hard to find specific moral guidance in religious scriptures. They were written long ago, survived as oral traditions, have been translated multiple times, and are open to multiple interpretations. (Anyone who has ever translated languages knows that literal interpretations are impossible.) Moreover, church traditions are ambiguous on many moral issues.

The key idea of the conservative view is that the fetus is a person with full moral rights. Most philosophers deny this claim because the necessary or sufficient conditions of personhood are notoriously difficult to ascertain and the fetus doesn't satisfy many, if any, of the conditions. The impartial view, backed by contemporary biology, is that a fetus is a potential person. But allowing for the sake of argument that the conservative view is the Christian view, then this must be supported by either church tradition or church scriptures. But is it?

The difficulty of deriving a prohibition against abortion from Christian scriptures is well-known since the issue doesn't arise in the Christian scriptures. There are a few Biblical passages quoted by conservatives to support the anti-abortion position, the most

Chapter 11 – Abortion

well-known is in Jeremiah: "Before I formed you in the womb I knew you, and before you were born I consecrated you." But, as anyone who has examined this passage knows, the sanctity of fetal life isn't being discussed here. Rather Jeremiah is asserting his authority as a prophet. (This is a classic example of seeking support in holy books for a position you already hold.)

Many other Biblical passages point to the more liberal view of abortion. Three times in the Bible (Genesis 38:24; Leviticus 21:9; Deuteronomy 22:20–21) the death penalty is recommended for women who have sex out-of-wedlock even though killing the women would kill their fetuses. (I don't think death is recommended for men who have such sex. I wonder why?) Furthermore, in Exodus 21, God prescribes death as the penalty for murder, whereas the penalty for causing a woman to miscarry is a fine. In the Old Testament, the fetus doesn't have personhood status. Thus there is no strong scriptural tradition in Christianity against abortion.

There also is no strong church tradition against abortion. The idea that the fetus is a person from the moment of conception is quite new in church tradition. St. Thomas Aquinas, the preeminent thinker in Catholicism, held that embryo didn't acquire a soul for several weeks into gestation—after the embryo had a human form. This position was officially accepted by the church at the Council of Vienne in 1312.

However, in the 17th century, scientists peering through primitive microscopes at fertilized eggs thought they saw tiny, perfectly formed people—what they called a "homunculus," or little man. Now if humans had a human shape from the moment of conception then it follows, from Aquinas, that it has a soul from the very beginning. This mistaken view of embryological development led to the Church changing its stand on abortion.

Of course, we now know there is no homunculus. We know that embryos start out as a cluster of cells, and human form comes later. But when the biological error was corrected, the church didn't revert to its earlier moral position. Instead, it held to the position it holds to this day, that the soul enters the embryo from conception, even though this view is based on a false view of the biological facts.

The point of all this isn't that the contemporary church's position is wrong—it may be right. The point is that the anti-abortion position doesn't clearly follow from either church tradition or scripture. What really happens when people suppose that religion demands a certain moral view is that they already have moral views, and then look to scripture or tradition to support those views. People's moral convictions aren't usually derived from their religion so much as superimposed on it. All of this suggests that true morality isn't based on religion but on reason and conscience. As Plato argued in his dialogue *Euthyphro*, things can't be right just because the gods command them, the gods must command them because they're right. And if that's the case then the gods have some reason for their commands, reasons that are intelligible to rational beings.

Thus we are led back to philosophical ethics. In the case of abortion, rational arguments either support the anti-abortion position or they do not. The vast majority of professional philosophers find those arguments seriously deficient, while the opposing arguments are philosophically robust. Still, this situation may change in the future.

6. American Politics and Abortion

There is much to say about the politics of all this, but there is no doubt much of the anti-abortion rhetoric in American society

Chapter 11 – Abortion

comes from a punitive, puritanical desire to punish people for having sex. Many are hypocritical on the issue, simultaneously opposing abortion as well as the only proven majors of reducing abortion—good sex education and readily available birth control. Of course, there are sincere people who oppose abortion because they think it is immoral too.

As for politicians, there is some sincere opposition among them, but for many (if not most) their public opposition is hypocritical and self-interested. Generally, they don't care about the issue—they care about the power and wealth derived from politics—but they feign concern while throwing red meat to their constituencies. And while they may be pro-birth, they clearly aren't pro-life, as evidenced by the fact that they vigorously oppose helping children after they are born by denying them education, health-care, economic opportunities, and the like.

In the end, rational discourse is the only violence-free way to resolve moral controversies in a morally pluralistic society. To the extent they can't be resolved, American secular democracy has traditionally allowed individuals to hold to their beliefs, but never to impose them on others unless clear harm was being done to others. (John Stuart Mill's "harm principle.") You can hold, practice, and advocate whatever religious or ethical beliefs you like as long as you don't use the coercive power of government to force others to believe or act likewise, and as long as you don't hurt others. (You can' t beat your children or kill heathens.)Whether religious people should be able to use the coercive power of the government to force others to act and believe accordingly sets a dangerous precedent unless one truly believes in theocracy.

Chapter 12 – Euthanasia and Biotechnology

Dogs don't have many advantages over people, but one of them is extremely important: euthanasia isn't forbidden by law in their case; animals have the right to a merciful death. ~ Milan Kundera

1. The Euthanasia Debate

Technology prolongs and sustains life artificially. Parallel to the question of when something becomes a person in the abortion debate, a central question in the euthanasia debate is when does one cease to be a person? If one is deemed no longer to be a person, then the question of their rights is less important.

What is death? Until recently the cessation of breathing or heartbeat defined death. Now machines maintain respiration and heartbeat even when there is no brain functioning. So increasingly brain death is the preferred definition.

Relevant to the discussion of death are: 1) philosophical concerns about what is a person; 2) physiological concerns about what criteria define death; and 3) methods used to determine physiological states. Moreover, the various definitions have a huge impact on moral decisions—if one is already dead, the moral situation is different than if one isn't.)

Another important distinction is between *ordinary* treatments that offer a hope of benefit without undue cost vs. *extraordinary* treatments that offer no hope of benefit at great cost. A difficulty here is that what was once extraordinary—say heart surgery—eventually becomes ordinary.

We can also differentiate between *killing* and *allowing to die*. The former refers to an act of commission (causing harm) that brings about death; the latter to an act of omission (permitting

Chapter 12 – Euthanasia and Biotechnology

harm) that brings on death. Defenders of the importance of the distinction argue that if we kill, we are the cause of death; whereas if we allow someone to die, the disease is the cause of death. Opponents argue the distinction isn't relevant.

A *narrow* definition of euthanasia (E) includes only killing as E; allowing to die isn't E. Proponents typically view E as wrong, but allowing to die as not wrong. A *broad* definition of E includes both killing (active E) and allowing to die (passive E). Proponents typically argue that both killing and letting die can be moral.

We can also distinguish between *voluntary* E—where the patient consents to treatment or non-treatment—and *non-voluntary* E—where someone other than the patient gives consent. In addition, sometimes the category of *involuntary* E describes cases where one doesn't consent and has not made their wishes known beforehand.

Another important category is *assisted suicide*, typically by a physician (PAS). This is similar to voluntary active E except that in PAS the physician doesn't kill patients, but enables it. The right to *refuse treatment* has been recognized in America since 1990. In addition, the use of living wills, durable power of attorney, advanced directives, and similar documents are now allowed.

Problematic euthanasia cases include the issue of defective newborns (DN). Here positions range from: 1) allowing to die in most circumstances; 2) allowing to die only when DN won't have meaningful lives; 3) never allow to die. (At the other extreme would be killing in most circumstances.)

2. Euthanasia is Wrong

In his article, The Wrongfulness of Euthanasia, J. Gay Williams rejects the view that "that if someone (and others) would be better off dead, then it must be all right to kill that person." For Gay-Williams euthanasia (E) is intentional or deliberate killing, not accidental killing or letting one die. Given his subsequent rejection of the notion of passive E, it's clear he is using the narrow definition of E. E is intentional killing only, in other words, it's active E. Passive E isn't E because one doesn't intend the person's death—it's a foreseeable, but unintended consequence. (I foresee my driving will wear out my tires, but I don't intend to wear them out by driving.) Here are his arguments:

The *argument from nature* may be reconstructed as follows:
1. Acts of euthanasia are contrary to our human nature.
2. If (1), then acts of euthanasia are a denial of human dignity.
3. If acts of euthanasia are a denial of human dignity, then euthanasia is morally wrong.
4. Therefore, euthanasia is morally wrong.

The *argument from self-interest* may be summarized as follows:
1. Acts of euthanasia contain the possibility that we will work against our own interests.
2. If (1), then acts of euthanasia are morally wrong.
3. Therefore, acts of euthanasia are morally wrong.

Support for (1): (a) Possibility of bad diagnosis/prognosis; (b) possibility of new medical procedures; (c) thinking euthanasia permissible may encourage one to give up too easily; (d) choose E because of our concern for others.

The *argument from practical effects* may be summarized as follows:
1. Cases of euthanasia could have a corrupting influence on doctors and nurses.
2. If (1), then acts of euthanasia are morally wrong.
3. Therefore, acts of euthanasia are morally wrong.

Chapter 12 – Euthanasia and Biotechnology

Support for 1: a) doctors and nurses might not try hard enough to save someone; and b) this may lead to involuntary E. (A "slippery slope" argument.)

3. Active and Passive Euthanasia

The late philosopher James Rachels (R) published one of the most salient pieces on the euthanasia debate in 1975 the New England Journal of Medicine titled "Active and Passive Euthanasia." Forty years later it's still considered a classic. Here is an outline of his argument.

Rachels argues that the distinction between active euthanasia (AE) and passive euthanasia (PE) is thought to be crucial. But this is mistaken. Why? In the first place, *AE is preferable to PE because it reduces suffering*. To understand this point R says that he understands, for example, saving all defective newborns, or destroying certain ones, for instance, a baby with down syndrome (DS) or with congenital defects for example. But he doesn't understand allowing them to die slowly and painfully. This middle position makes no sense. Why?

First, *the distinction between active and passive euthanasia leads to making life and death decisions on irrelevant grounds*. For example, intestinal blockage allows us to let a DS baby die, but without the blockage, we would have to kill it. But the blockage is irrelevant. The issue is whether the DS baby should live. Thus the distinction between AE and PE leads to us thinking intestinal blockage was an important moral consideration. But it isn't.

Second, *killing isn't worse than letting die*. Consider: 1) Smith drowns his cousin for money; and 2) Jones lets his cousin drown for money. It doesn't seem there is any moral difference between the two cases. Similarly, whether you kill or let die for a good motive—say to relieve suffering—the act is right or wrong independent of how you brought death about. In both cases, the intent or motive is primarily to terminate life (and relieve suffering or costs). We tend to think killing is worse than letting die because usually bad guys kill and physicians let die. But this doesn't mean that there is something intrinsic to killing which is worse than letting die.

Counter-argument – In PE the physician doesn't do anything and the disease kills the patient. In AE the physician does something to kill the patient.

Rachels response – 1) Physicians do do something when they practice PE—they let people die. That is a type of action. 2) It's bad to cause someone's death because death is ordinarily thought bad for them. But if death has been deemed preferable, then bringing about death is no longer bad. 3) Physicians may have to go along with the law, but the distinction can't be defended philosophically. [This is a flawlessly reasoned piece, and I believe its argument is increasingly winning the day.]

4. Voluntary Active Euthanasia

Dan Brock (B), in his essay "Voluntary Active Euthanasia," discusses voluntary active euthanasia in cases "where the motive of those who perform it's to respect the wishes of the patient and to provide the patient with a "good death…"

The Central Ethical Argument for Voluntary Active Euthanasia

The values supporting voluntary active euthanasia "are individual self- determination or autonomy and individual well- being." Self-determination refers to persons being free to make decisions about their own lives. [Rather than governments, religious organizations, political groups, strangers, etc.] And this autonomy ought to extend to the end of life when persons worry about suffering and the loss of dignity. Individual well-being refers to situations in which

Chapter 12 – Euthanasia and Biotechnology

individuals decide that "life is no longer considered a benefit by the patient, but has now become a burden." In other words, their well-being is best served by dying. However, this doesn't imply that physicians must perform this act against their conscience.

Potential Good Consequences of Permitting Euthanasia

1) Respect individual autonomy (of about 50,000 persons a year in the US in this situation; 2) give reassurance to those who may want euthanasia in the future; and 3) it will relieve vast amounts of suffering.

Potential Bad Consequences of Permitting Euthanasia

B list 3 arguments: 1) performing is incompatible with the "moral center" of being a physician and thus patients would fear their physicians. B replies that patients shouldn't fear that their physicians will kill them, since E would be voluntary and the moral center of medicine should be self-determination and individual well-being, not preserving life when persons have deemed they no longer want that. 2) E would weaken respect for life. B responds that he is skeptical because: a) passive euthanasia had no such consequences; and b) euthanasia would only be relevant in a small minority of deaths. 3) Legalizing voluntary euthanasia would lead down a slippery slope to involuntary euthanasia. B responds that this is the "last refuge of conservative defenders of the status quo." When all your arguments against something have been defeated you simply say that this something will lead to something else.

While it's possible that doing x will lead to bad consequence y, that isn't enough of a reason not to do x. We don't want to know if this is possible, but if it's plausible. And no one had done this. B suggests a number of safeguards to minimize the chance of abuse. However, the idea that one must be terminally ill—like the law demands in Oregon and Washington in the US—doesn't sufficiently respect self-determination. There is no justification for disallowing people access to euthanasia in cases in which they are suffering severely but not terminal. Still, B says that OR and WA can serve as test cases for such laws. Better still to look to a system like in the Netherlands, which has had much more liberal laws regarding euthanasia on the books for decades without significant problems.

5. David Hume on Suicide

David Hume (1711-1776) was a Scottish philosopher, economist, historian and one of the most famous figures in the history of Western philosophy and the Scottish Enlightenment. Hume begins his essay on suicide like this:

> One considerable advantage that arises from Philosophy, consists in the sovereign antidote which it affords to superstition and false religion…when sound Philosophy has once gained possession of the mind, superstition is effectually excluded; and one may fairly affirm, that her triumph over this enemy is more complete than over most of the vices and imperfections incident to human nature.

Philosophy is an antidote to the superstition and irrationalism that make our lives miserable. The superstitious can't even take refuge from their misery in sleep because they are haunted by their dreams; nor can they take refuge in their death, even if they are quite miserable or in pain since they fear offending the gods. Therefore superstition forces them to stay alive, even when dying would be preferable. When fear of death is joined by superstition the result "deprives men of all power over their lives…" We fear bringing about death even though it would often be better to do so.

Chapter 12 – Euthanasia and Biotechnology

Hume examines suicide "to restore men to their native liberty …" He has in mind the superstition that prevents people from committing suicide when in pain. Hume distinguishes the laws by which the gods govern nature and the laws by which humans govern themselves. Just as nature carries on without considering the interests of humans, so humans may use the power the gods have given them regarding their own happiness. People don't incur the wrath of a god by exercising their will since the gods have given them this power. If it would be against the gods' province to choose to commit suicide, then it would be against the province of the gods to preserve life by saving someone from an oncoming boulder.

Similarly, since according to the laws of nature an insect can destroy human life, it would be strange if humans weren't granted such powers regarding their own lives. Hume believes that the gods must have given us the power to escape a bad life. Consider that if our enemies hurt us, most will allow us to fight back. Why then demand that I resign myself to inaction if threatened by pain and suffering? So Hume argues that people's lives are their own, to dispose of as they choose because the gods have given us this power. That is why we dam rivers and create vaccines, or act as heroes and risk our lives; we use the power the gods have given us to change the world.

Hume argues that committing suicide does no harm to society. He also says that when we are dead, we no longer receive benefits from society, and hence we no longer have obligations. But even if we did have obligations, surely they are limited. If we aren't obligated to do a small good for society at great expense to ourselves, then we aren't obligated to suffer greatly for some small benefit to society. If I am old and infirm I may quit my job, thereby ceasing contributing to society. So why may I not quit life? And if the continuation of my life is a burden to society, then I should be praised for ending it. Or if you are about to be tortured for crimes against society, wouldn't putting yourself to death be in the public's interest? That wouldn't invade the realm of providence anymore than those who ordered the torture did.

In brief, Hume argued that we should generally respect individual autonomy, including a person's choice of when to die.

6. Worse Off Alive

In a 1994 article in the American Philosophical Association's Newsletter On Philosophy and Medicine, the philosopher John Messerly penned an article entitled, "Worse Off Alive: Reply to Garcia." Here are some salient excerpts.

The goal of J.L.A Garcia's article, "Better Off Dead,"(Volume 92, No. 1, pp. 82-85) "is to cast doubt on the doctrines that someone's dying can be a good thing for that person, that some lives aren't worth living, and that there can be a right to die." Thus, he argues, we are never "better off dead" and that nearly all human lives are worth living. He also implies—but never specifically argues—that there is no right to die. I argue that, though we aren't "better off dead," we may be "worse off alive," when enduring extraordinary suffering. I also argue that lives deprived of certain goods aren't worth living. Let us examine Garcia's arguments in turn.

According to Garcia, euthanasia proponents deem death an instrumental good because it relieves a patient's suffering. But instrumental goods, he argues, are good only when they "make our lives go better," and being free from anxiety, or physical pain "is good inasmuch as it yields a less troubled life." Since causing or allowing someone to die doesn't make their lives go better, it isn't an instrumental good. In short, dying brings about no good for a person—since dead persons don't exist—and thus, one can't be "better off dead."

Chapter 12 – Euthanasia and Biotechnology

Garcia is partly correct. It's never better to be dead in the sense that one's life benefits or improves by dying, and therefore if death is non-existence as he seems to suppose, no good or bad comes from being dead. The problem with this argument is twofold: 1) it reduces to the self-evident and trivial assertion that non-existent persons can't experience good; and 2) it misconstrues the issue. Few persons who desire to be relieved from excruciating suffering believe they will gain from their death by experiencing some benefit, except possibly in an afterlife. What they obviously do believe is that, in their present condition, they are "worse off alive," and this justifies euthanasia for them. In their condition, they prefer death to life because life offers so little, not because death offers some gain or benefit.

In certain cases Garcia seems to agree: "When we permissibly withhold or terminate treatment in such cases, it's because we judge that the kind of life that aggressive treatment could secure the patient isn't so great a good as to require us to secure it at staggering cost to the patient herself or to others." Presumably, the cases to which he refers are those that employ extraordinary means, though he doesn't explain why this rationale applies only to these cases. Nonetheless, if life isn't the only good, as he admits, and the kinds of life secured by certain treatments aren't good enough to be preferred to death, then we are sometimes "worse off alive."

Next Garcia turns to the claim that some lives aren't "worthwhile." This claim, he argues, results from the disparity between healthy, highly educated, refined, and economically advantaged bioethicists, and the dying. These professionals judge the quality of life of the dying to be quite minimal, overlooking many similarities between themselves and the dying, particularly their shared existential despair. Such considerations [should] caution us against hasty generalizations about the value of human lives. Who is to say that our lives, projects, and goals are valuable? And if we can't be certain about the value of our own lives, how can we be so sure about the value of the lives of others?

This argument is problematic for at least two reasons: 1) it applies only to those advocating non-voluntary active euthanasia; and 2) what follows from it's that we should reject proxy judgments of the value of individual lives. But it doesn't follow that it's never better to die or that all lives are worth living. What he has shown is that by resisting generalizations and proxy judgments we respect human autonomy, a fundamental value according to Garcia, "even if the choices we make are often disastrous." Thus ... has failed to show that all lives are worth living.

Garcia concludes by "rejecting the suggestions that it might be better for someone to die and that her life might be improved by her death." He correctly assumes that our lives don't improve when we die because then, obviously, we no longer [have] experience[s]. And if life is a good so great that no possible agony, suffering, evil, pain, or torment negate its value, then life is always preferable to death.

However, most ordinary individuals disagree. They applaud the advanced directives for health care, sign their living wills, and ask their spouses, friends, sons or daughters to act as their surrogates. They choose to forgo the remainder of lives deprived of those things that make life valuable—the ability to love, think, touch, reflect, and remember—for the uncertainty of death. They prefer not to debase human life or glorify suffering but to exercise human autonomy. For those who believe there is meaning in the most excruciating forms of physical pain and dementia—let them go their way. But for those of us who believe that, at least sometimes, we are "worse off alive"—let us go our way.

Chapter 12 – Euthanasia and Biotechnology

7. Against the Use of Biotechnology

In "Stem Cells, Biotechnology and Human Rights" Paul Lauritzen, a professor of Theology and Religious Studies at John Carroll University near Cleveland, discusses two broad concerns posed by stem cell research and related biotechnological interventions. *The first* has to do with the prospect of transforming the contours of human life in fairly dramatic ways. The *second* has to do with our attitudes toward the natural world.

As we move to change the meaning of human embodiment in fundamental ways, including the possibility of eroding species boundaries, we need to ask whether we are prepared to reduce the entire natural world to the status of artifact. (Is that what we would be doing? If so, is that bad?) These concerns raise questions about the meaning of human rights in a post-human future.

Despite the overwhelming questions of embryo status, ultimately the fundamental question raised by stem cell research isn't about the embryo. Instead, it's about the future toward which biotechnology beckons us. Does contemporary biotechnology, including stem cell research, open the door to a post-human future? (It obviously does, but is this bad, and if so why?)

Others raise this question explicitly when they discuss the combination of genetic engineering and stem cell therapy. They suggest that xeno-transplantation forces us to confront the prospect of transgressing species boundaries. When a graft involves genetically engineered stem cells from another species, questions are raised not just about the ontological status of the graft recipient, but about the illnesses to which the biomedical technology is responding.

(Do species differ in degree or kind? If they differ only in degree, as modern biology maintains, then the transgressing species boundary argument makes little sense. And even if we do change the species, why is this bad? Perhaps Lauritzen's argument is a sophisticated version of the "yuch" argument—I oppose this stuff because it seems yucky!)

Questions about the implications of pursuing stem cell research haven't been systematically asked or answered. Given the potential for alleviating human suffering embedded in the prospects of stem cell research, it isn't surprising that there appears to be widespread and largely uncritical acceptance of such research. Nevertheless, if the promise of stem cell research is as revolutionary as is often claimed, we are going to need a much more expansive discussion of stem cell research than we have had.

If stem cell research leads to therapies that change the natural contours of human life, it will unsettle our ethical commitments, including the very notion of a human right, and encourage us to see the entire natural world, the human body along with it, as having the status only of material to be manipulated.

8. In Defense of Cloning Humans

Michael Tooley's article "Moral Status of Cloning Humans" defends human cloning. Here is a brief outline of the article with a bit of commentary identified by parenthesis.

SECTION 1 –Cloning might be wrong intrinsically because: 1) the right of a person to a genetically unique nature; and 2) the right of a person to a future that is, in a certain sense, open.

Regarding 1 – Is it important to be unique? If there were another you on a distant planet does that diminish your worthiness?

Two persons could be identical because of deterministic law (genes and environment), or by chance (identical twins). Most people aren't bothered by the latter, but by the former. If bothered

Chapter 12 – Euthanasia and Biotechnology

by the former, is that because such persons would not be unique, or is one bothered because they don't like determinism? Tooley thinks its determinism they don't like, not the lack of uniqueness. But they should have no worries since cloning—even less than identical twins reared together—doesn't imply genetic determinism (and doesn't produce identical people.)

Do persons then have a right to a unique genome? The case of twins suggests they don't, as no one worries that there are twins or thinks it wrong to have twins. But is there some right violated by being a clone? It seems not. One's individuality isn't threatened because someone else shares your genome. (Again that implies that genetic determinism is true, but we aren't genetically determined.)

Or consider that if the gods had to choose between a) evolution; b) an original pair who would mate, or c) an original pair who would reproduce perfect clones of themselves forever. Might not the gods have rejected the former as too random, and chose the latter instead? Would this last world be worse than the others, or much better? Tooley thinks it would have been better. This suggests there isn't anything crucial about genetic uniqueness.

Regarding 2 – We might think certain futures aren't open to us because someone who preceded us did or didn't do certain things. Tooley suggests such knowledge would be helpful since we wouldn't attempt to do impossible or extremely unlikely things based upon knowledge of our genome. Or, if one thought themselves constrained by their genome, they would be wrong, as the case of identical twins shows. (Again, genetic potentials, propensities, or proclivities don't imply genetic determinism.) Thus the arguments against cloning are unconvincing.

Philosophical Ethics: Theory And Practice

SECTION 2 – In support of cloning Tooley offers the following:

1. We would gain scientific knowledge about nature vs. nurture debate. Such knowledge would be potentially beneficial to society and child rearing;
2. We could clone persons who have made significant contributions to society;
3. We can increase the chances that one will be happy and healthy;
4. It will improve and inform the relationship for both children and parents—since the parent will better recall what it was to be that child;
5. It would help infertile couples who couldn't otherwise have children;
6. It will allow homosexual couples to have their own children; and
7. It would save lives (primarily by the ability to clone perfectly compatible organs.)

SECTION 3 – Objections to the Cloning of Humans

Still, even if the arguments against cloning are weak—as the first section demonstrated—and there are multiple benefits to cloning—as the second section argued—cloning might still be wrong because of some bad consequences that might follow its adoption.

Arguments against cloning and responses to those arguments -

1. Creating mindless organ banks is wrong because you are killing a person, or because you aren't allowing a person to have a brain or soul, or because it's killing a potential person.

    Response – Tooley rejects all of these objections. There are no convincing reasons to think that embryos, brainless organs, or potential people are people. Furthermore, while

Chapter 12 – Euthanasia and Biotechnology

some may think organ banks are ghoulish, not using them allows innocent people to die who would otherwise not die. Thus to advocate against cloning is to recommend a course of action that will result in the death of many innocent people. (Remember also that in practice we're talking about cells being directed to develop into a pancreas, liver, heart, etc. Not whole bodies hanging on hooks in chambers as in the movies.)

2. Cloning violates the rights of clones to a genetically unique or open future.

    Response – This objection has already dealt with.

3. Brave New World scenarios such as human beings will be cloned to serve as slaves, soldiers in the dictator's army, etc.

    Response – Such scenarios aren't plausible. Would society suddenly change their mind about the immorality of slavery because of genetic engineering? Would a dictator who couldn't conscript his own army undertake a cloning project so that in twenty years he had the army he wanted? Not likely. (Remember you must show not that something is possible but that it's plausible.)

4. Cloning will cause psychological distress because clones will think their uniqueness compromised or future constrained.

    Response – The beliefs that give rise to such distress are, as we have seen, false; and they are also irrational since, as we have seen, genetic determinism is false. But we shouldn't be constrained by the irrational beliefs of others. Moreover, these irrational beliefs will cease when cloning becomes familiar.

5. We use children—treat them as means to an end—when we clone them to save another child.

   Response – Tooley thinks it unlikely that parents would be less likely to care or love their offspring in such situations.

6. Cloning interferes with autonomy.

   Response – If my child is cloned with a genetic capability or potential to be intellectuals, that doesn't mean they have to be. The same if they are disposed to be intellectuals; they still don't have to be. In addition, is it really wrong to want children who won't suffer from genetic diseases? Finally, If cloning to produce children with certain traits is wrong, then so are almost all child-rearing practices.

SECTION 4 – Conclusion

Human cloning is generally acceptable and potentially very beneficial for society.

9. Against Genetic Engineering

Michael J. Sandel, a professor of philosophy at Harvard, makes his case against human enhancement in his article, "The Case against Perfection." Here is a brief outline of the piece.

Genetic engineering will improve the species, but some of it seems yucky. To understand this we need to consider "the moral status of nature, and …the proper stance of human beings toward the given world." Why is genetic engineering so bad? "The problem with eugenics and genetic engineering is that they represent the one-sided triumph of willfulness over giftedness, of dominion over reverence, of molding over beholding

With genetic engineering:

Chapter 12 – Euthanasia and Biotechnology

- We won't be humble (about our gifts): "If bioengineering made the myth of the " self- made man" come true, it would be difficult to view our talents as gifts for which we are indebted rather than achievements for which we are responsible."

- We will be too responsible (for human fate): "As humility gives way, responsibility expands to daunting proportions. We attribute less to chance and more to choice… The more we become masters of our genetic endowments, the greater the burden we bear for the talents we have and the way we perform… A domain once governed by fate has now become an arena of choice." (Is this true? And if it is, is it bad that it's true?)

- We will feel less solidarity (with others): "…genetic enhancement, if routinely practiced, would make it harder to foster the moral sentiments that social solidarity requires." (I don't see why this is true.)

Objections

1. "Some may complain that it's overly religious; others may object that it's unpersuasive in consequentialist terms." Response – "These various understandings of the sacred all insist that we value nature and the living beings within it as more than mere instruments; to act otherwise displays a lack of reverence, a failure of respect."

2. "But those who care more about gaining a competitive edge for their children or themselves may decide that the benefits to be gained from genetic enhancement outweigh its allegedly adverse effects on social institutions and moral sentiments." Response – "My concern with enhancement isn't as individual vice but as habit of mind and way of being." Sandel concludes:

The bigger stakes are of two kinds. One involves the fate of human goods embodied in important social practice—norms of unconditional love and an openness to the unbidden, in the case of parenting; the celebration of natural talents and gifts in athletic and artistic endeavors; humility in the face of privilege, and a willingness to share the fruits of good fortune through institutions of social solidarity. The other involves our orientation to the world that we inhabit, and the kind of freedom to which we aspire. ..But changing our nature to fit the world, rather than the other way around, is actually the deepest form of disempowerment. It distracts us from reflecting critically on the world, and deadens the impulse to social and political improvement. Rather than employ our new genetic powers to straighten 'the crooked timber of humanity,' we should do what we can to create social and political arrangements more hospitable to the gifts and limitations of imperfect human beings…

Chapter 13 – Death

This is the terror: to have emerged from nothing, to have a name, consciousness of self, deep inner feelings, an excruciating inner yearning for life and self-expression—and with all this yet to die.
~ Ernest Becker

1. Is Death Bad For Us?

Is death good or bad for us? Vincent Barry, professor emeritus at Bakersfield College, carefully considered this question in his 2007 textbook, *Philosophical Thinking About Death and Dying*. I reconstruct his discussion in what follows.

Is Death Bad? – One of Barry's main concerns is whether death is or isn't bad for us. As he notes, the argument that death isn't bad derives from Epicurus' aphorism: "When I am, death isn't; and when death is, I am not." Epicurus taught that fear in general, and fear of the gods and death in particular was evil.

Consequently, using reason to rid ourselves of these fears was a primary goal of his speculative thinking. A basic assumption of his thought was a materialistic psychology in which mind was composed of atoms, and death the dispersal of those atoms. Thus death isn't then bad for us since something can be bad only if we are affected by it, but we have no sensation after death and thus being dead can't be bad for us. Note that this doesn't imply that the process or the prospect of dying can't be bad for us—they can—nor does Epicurus deny that we might prefer life to death. His argument is that being dead isn't bad for the one who has died.

Epicurus' argument relies on two separate assumptions—the experience requirement and the existence requirement. The *experience requirement* states roughly:

1. Harm to someone is bad for them. For something to be bad for someone, it must be experienced by them.
2. Death is a state of no experience.
3. Therefore death can't be bad for someone.

The *existence requirement* can be summarized thus:

1. A person can be harmed only if they exist.
2. A dead person doesn't exist.
3. Therefore a dead person can't be harmed.

As we will see, counter-arguments attack one of the two requirements. Either they try to show that someone can be harmed without experiencing the harm, or that someone who is dead can still be harmed.

One noted philosopher who attacks the Epicurean view is Thomas Nagel. In his essay "Death," Nagel argues that death is bad for someone who dies even if that person doesn't consciously survive death. According to this deprivation theory, death is bad for persons who die because of the good things their deaths deprive them of. However, if death is bad because it limits the possibility of future goods, is death not then good in limiting the possibility of future evils? So the possibility of future goods doesn't by itself show that death is bad; to show that one would have to show that a future life would be worth living, that is, that it would contain more good than bad. But how can any deprivation theory explain how it's bad for us to be deprived of something if we don't experience that deprivation? How can what we don't know hurt us?

In reply Nagel argues that we can be harmed without being aware of it. An intelligent man reduced to the state of infancy by a brain injury has suffered a great misfortune, even if unaware of, and

Chapter 13 – Death

contented in his injurious state. Nagel argues that many states that we don't experience can be bad for us—the betrayal of a friend, the loss of reputation, or the unfaithfulness of a spouse. And just as an adult reduced to infancy is the subject of a misfortune, so too is one who is dead. But critics wonder who it's that is the subject of this harm? Even if it's bad to be deprived of certain goods, who is it that is deprived? How can the dead be harmed? There apparently is no answer to this question.

And there is another problem. While the deprivation argument may explain why death is bad for us, it follows from it that being denied prenatal existence would also be bad. Yet we don't ordinarily consider ourselves harmed by not having been born sooner. How can we explain this asymmetry?

Epicurus argued that this asymmetry couldn't be explained, and we should feel indifferent to death just as we do to prenatal existence. This sentiment was echoed by Mark Twain:

> Annihilation has no terrors for me, because I have already tried it before I was born—a hundred million years—and I have suffered more in an hour, in this life, than I remember to have suffered in the whole hundred million years put together. There was a peace, a serenity, an absence of all sense of responsibility, an absence of worry, an absence of care, grief, perplexity; and the presence of a deep content and unbroken satisfaction in that hundred million years of holiday which I look back upon with a tender longing and with a grateful desire to resume when the opportunity comes.

In reply, the deprivationists argue that we don't have to hold symmetrical views about prenatal and postnatal experience—claiming instead that asymmetrical views are consistent with ordinary experience. To see why consider the following. Would you rather have suffered a long surgical operation last year or undergo a short one tomorrow? Would you rather have had pleasure yesterday, or pleasure tomorrow? In both cases we have more concern with the future than the past; we are less interested in past events than in future ones. Death in the future deprives us of future goods, whereas prenatal nonexistence deprived us of past goods about which we are now indifferent. For all these reasons Barry concludes that death is probably bad and a fear of it is rational.

2. Death Is Bad For Us

Given that death is probably bad for us, what then do we do, assuming death is inevitable? Perhaps we should just be optimistic. We really haven't anything to lose by being optimistic and, given the current reality of death, this is a wise option. William James suggested as much in his essay "The Will to Believe,"

> We stand on a mountain pass in the midst of whirling snow and blinding mist, through which we get glimpses now and then of paths which may be deceptive. If we stand still we shall be frozen to death. If we take the wrong road we shall be dashed to pieces. We don't certainly know whether there is any right one. What must we do? 'Be strong and of a good courage.' Act for the best, hope for the best, and take what comes. ... If death ends all, we can't meet death better.

But even such stirring words don't change the fact that death is bad. Bad because it puts an end to something which at its best is beautiful; bad because all the knowledge and insight and wisdom of that person is lost; bad because of the harm it does to the living; bad because it causes people to be unconcerned about the future

Chapter 13 – Death

beyond their short lifespan; and bad because we know in our bones, that if we had the choice, and if our lives were going well, we would choose to on. That death is generally bad—especially so for the physically, morally, and intellectually vigorous—is nearly self-evident.

But most of all, death is bad because it renders completely meaningful lives impossible. It's true that longer lives don't guarantee meaningful ones, but all other things being equal, longer lives contain the possibility of more meaning than shorter ones. (Both the quality and the quantity of a life are relevant to its meaning; both are necessary though not sufficient conditions for meaning.) An infinite life can be without meaning, but a life of no duration, a non-existent life, is by definition meaningless. A happy, healthy, well-lived finite life of twenty years may contain a lot of meaning, but an identically well-lived life would be more meaningful if it were lived for another twenty or forty or eighty or ten-thousand years. While there are no guarantees, the possibility of greater meaning–the total meaning of a life–increases proportionately with the length of a lifetime.

Yes, there are indeed fates worse than death, and in some circumstances, death may be welcomed even if it extinguishes the further possibility of meaning. Nevertheless, death is one of the worst fates that can befall us, despite the consolations offered by the deathists—the lovers of death. We may become bored with eternal consciousness, but as long as we can end our lives if we want, as long as we can opt out of immortality, who wouldn't want the option to live forever?

Only if we can choose whether to live or die are we really free. Our lives aren't our own if they can be taken from us without our consent, and, to the extent death can be delayed or prevented, further possibilities for meaning ensue. Perhaps with our hard-earned knowledge, we can slay death, thereby opening up the possibility for more meaningful lives. This is perhaps the fundamental imperative for our species. For now, the best we can do is to remain optimistic in the face of the great tragedy that is death.

3. How Science May Defeat Death

If death is our end, then all we can do is die and hope for the best. But perhaps we don't have to die. Many scientists now believe that humans can overcome death and achieve immortality through the use of future technologies. But how will we do this?

The first way we might achieve physical immortality is by conquering our biological limitations—we age, become diseased, and suffer trauma. Aging research, while woefully underfunded, has yielded positive results. Average life expectancies have tripled since ancient times, increasing by more than fifty percent in the industrial world in the last hundred years, and most scientists think we will continue to extend our life-spans. We know that some jellyfish and bacteria are essentially immortal, and the bristlecone pine may be too. There is no thermodynamic necessity for senescence—aging is a presumed byproduct of evolution — although why mortality was selected for remains a mystery. Yet some scientists believe we can conquer aging altogether—in the next few decades with sufficient investment—most notably the Cambridge researcher Aubrey de Grey.

If we do unlock the secrets of aging, we will simultaneously defeat other diseases as well, since many of them are symptoms of aging. Many researchers now consider aging itself to be a disease which progresses as you age. There are a number of strategies that could render disease mostly inconsequential. Nanotechnology may give us nanobot cell-repair machines and robotic blood cells;

Chapter 13 – Death

biotechnology may supply replacement tissues and organs; genetics may offer genetic medicine and engineering, and full-fledged genetic engineering could make us impervious to disease.

Trauma is a more intransigent problem from the biological perspective, although it too could be defeated through some combination of cloning, regenerative medicine, and genetic engineering. We can even imagine that your physicality could be recreated from a bit of your DNA, and other technologies could then fast forward your regenerated body to the age of your traumatic death, where a backup file containing your experiences and memories would be implanted in your brain. Even the dead may be resuscitated if they have undergone the process of cryonics—preserving organisms at very low temperatures in glass-like states. Ideally these clinically dead would be brought back to life when technology is sufficiently advanced. This may now be science fiction, but if nanotechnology fulfills its promise, there is a good chance that cryonics will succeed.

In addition to biological strategies for eliminating death, there are a number of technological scenarios for immortality which utilize advanced brain scanning techniques, artificial intelligence, and robotics. The most prominent scenarios have been advanced by the futurist Ray Kurzweil, who argues that the exponential growth of computing power, combined with advances in other technologies, will make it possible to upload the contents of one's consciousness into a virtual reality. This could be accomplished by cybernetics, whereby hardware would be gradually installed in the brain until the entire brain was running on that hardware, or via scanning the brain and simulating or transferring its contents to a sufficiently advanced computer. Either way, we would no longer be living in a physical world.

Philosophical Ethics: Theory And Practice

In fact, we may already be living in a computer simulation. The Oxford philosopher and futurist Nick Bostrom argues that advanced civilizations may have created computer simulations containing individuals with artificial intelligence and we might unknowingly be in such a simulation. Bostrom concludes that one of the following must be the case: civilizations never have the technology to run simulations; they have the technology but decided not to use it, or we almost certainly live in a simulation.

If we don't like the idea of being immortal in a virtual reality—or we don't like the idea that we may already be in one—we could upload our brain to a genetically engineered body if we like the feel of flesh, or to a robotic body if we like the feel of silicon or whatever materials comprised the robotic body. Along these lines MIT's Rodney Brooks envisions the merger of human flesh and machines, whereby humans slowly incorporate technology into their bodies, thus becoming more machine-like and indestructible. So a cyborg future may await us.

An evolutionary perspective underlies all these speculative scenarios. Once we embrace that perspective, it's easy to imagine that *our descendants will resemble us about as much as we do the amino acids from which we sprang.* Our knowledge is growing exponentially and, given eons of time for future innovation, it's easy to envisage that humans will defeat death and evolve in unimaginable ways. Remember that our evolution is no longer moved by the painstakingly slow process of Darwinian evolution—where bodies exchange information through genes—but by cultural evolution—where brains exchange information through memes. The most prominent feature of cultural evolution is the exponentially increasing pace of technological evolution—an evolution that may soon culminate in a *technological singularity*.

Chapter 13 – Death

The technological singularity, an idea first proposed by the mathematician Vernor Vinge, refers to the hypothetical future emergence of greater than human intelligence. Since the capabilities of such intelligences are difficult for our minds to comprehend, the singularity is seen as an event horizon beyond which the future becomes impossible to understand or predict. Nevertheless, we may surmise that this intelligence explosion will lead to increasingly powerful minds that will solve the problem of death.

But why conquer death? Why is death bad? It's bad because it ends something which at its best is good; because it puts an end to our projects; because the wisdom and knowledge of a person is lost at death; because it harms the living; because it causes apathy about the future beyond our short life-span; because it renders fully meaningful lives impossible; and because we know that if we had the choice, and if our lives were going well, we would choose to live on. That death is generally bad—especially for the physically and intellectually vigorous—is nearly self-evident.

Yes, there are indeed fates worse than death, and in some circumstances, death may be welcomed. Nevertheless for most of us most of the time, death is one of the worst fates that can befall us. That is why we think that suicide and murder and starvation and cancer are bad things. That is why we cry at funerals.

4. Death Should Be Optional

Today there are serious thinkers—Ray Kurzweil, Hans Moravec, Michio Kaku, Marshall Brain, Aubrey de Grey, Elon Musk, Stephen Hawking and others—who foresee that technology may enable humans to defeat death. There are also dissenters who argue that this is exceedingly unlikely. And there are those like Bill Joy who think that such technologies are technologically feasible but morally reprehensible.

As a non-scientist, I am not qualified to evaluate scientific claims about what science can and can't do. What I can say is that plausible scenarios for overcoming death have now appeared. This leads to the following questions: If individuals could choose immortality, should they? Should societies fund and promote research to defeat death?

The question regarding individuals has a straightforward answer—we should respect the right of autonomous individuals to choose for themselves. If an effective pill that stops or reverses aging becomes available at your local pharmacy, then you should be free to use it. My guess is that such a pill would be wildly popular! (Consider what people spend on vitamins and other elixirs on the basis of little or no evidence of their efficacy.) Or if, as you approach death, you are offered the opportunity to have your consciousness transferred to your younger cloned body, a genetically engineered body, a robotic body, or into a virtual reality, you should be free to do so. I believe that nearly everyone will use such technologies once they are demonstrated effective. But if individuals prefer to die in the hope that the gods will revive them in a paradise, thereby granting them reprieve from everlasting torment, then we should respect that too. Individuals should be free to end their lives even after death has become optional for them.

The argument about whether a society should fund and promote the research relevant to eliminating death is more complex. Societies currently invest vast sums on entertainment rather than scientific research; although the latter is a clearly a better societal investment. Ultimately the arguments for and against immortality must speak for themselves, but we reiterate that once science and technology have extended life significantly, or defeated death

Chapter 13 – Death

altogether, the point will be moot. By then almost everyone will choose to live as long as possible. In fact, many people do that now, at great cost, and often gaining only a few additional months of bad health. Imagine then how quickly they will choose life over death when the techniques are proven to lead to longer, healthier lives. As for the naysayers, they will get used to new technologies just like they did to previous ones.

Nonetheless, the virtual inevitability of advanced technologies to extend life doesn't imply their desirability, and many thinkers have campaigned actively and vehemently against utilizing such options. The defenders of death advocate maintaining the status quo with its daily dose of 150,000 deaths worldwide. Prominent among such thinkers are Leon Kass, who chaired George W. Bush's Council on Bioethics from 2001-2005, Francis Fukuyama, a Senior Fellow at the Center on Democracy, Development and the Rule of Law at Stanford, and Bill McKibbon, the Schumann Distinguished Scholar at Middlebury College.

Kass opposes euthanasia, human cloning, and embryonic stem cell research and was an early opponent of in vitro fertilization, which he thought would obscure truths about human life and society. (IVF had none of the dire consequences that Kass predicted; today the technology now goes mostly unnoticed.) One of Kass' main concerns is with the enhancement capability of biotechnology, which he fears will become a substitute for traditional human virtues. His concerns about modifying our biological inheritance extend to his worries about life extension. He values the natural cycle of life and views death as a desirable end—mortality, he says, is a blessing in disguise.

Fukuyama argues that biotechnology will alter human nature beyond recognition with terrible consequences. One would be the undermining of liberal democracy due to radical inequality between those who had access to such technologies and those who didn't. (Although there is plenty of social and economic inequality around today.) At an even more fundamental level, Fukuyama worries that the consequences of modifying humans are unknown. Should human beings really want to control their very natures? Fukuyama argues that we should be humble about such matters or "we may unwittingly invite the transhumanists to deface humanity with their genetic bulldozers and psychotropic shopping malls.

McKibbon admits the allure of technological utopia, knowing that it will be hard to resist, but he fears that the richness of human life would be lost in a post-human world. Even if we were godlike, spending our time meditating on the meaning of the cosmos or reflecting on our own consciousness like Aristotle's god, McKibbon says he would not trade his life for such an existence. He wouldn't want to be godlike, preferring instead to smell the fragrant leaves, feel the cool breeze, and see the fall colors. Yes, there is pain, suffering, cruelty, and death in the world, but this world is enough. "To call this world enough isn't to call it perfect or fair or complete or easy. But enough, just enough. And us in it."

There is a lot to say against all these views, but one wonders why these thinkers see human nature as sacrosanct. Is our nature so sacred that we should be apologists for it? Isn't it arrogant to think so highly of ourselves? This human nature produced what Hegel lampooned as "the slaughter-bench at which the happiness of peoples, the wisdom of States, and the virtue of individuals have been victimized." Surely we can do a better than what was created by genetic mutations and environmental selection.

Still, we must concede something to these warnings. The same technologies that may make us immortal are also the ones that bring robotic police and unmanned planes. Yet there is no way to assure that we will not suffer a nightmarish future no matter how

Chapter 13 – Death

we proceed. There is no risk-free way to proceed. With greater knowledge comes greater power, and with greater power comes the possibility of making life better or worse. The future with all its promises and perils will come regardless—all we can do is do our best.

The defense of immortality against such attacks has been undertaken most thoroughly by the recent intellectual and cultural movement known as *transhumanism*, which affirms the possibility and desirability of using technology to eliminate aging and overcome all other human limitations. Adopting an evolutionary perspective, transhumanists maintain that humans are in a relatively early phase of their development. They agree with humanism—that human beings matter and that reason, freedom, and tolerance make the world better—but emphasizes that we can become more than human by changing ourselves. This involves employing high-tech methods to transform the species and direct our own evolution, as opposed to relying on biological evolution or low-tech methods like education and training.

If science and technology develop sufficiently, this would lead to a stage where humans would no longer be recognized as human, but better described as post-human. But why would people want to transcend human nature? Because

> they yearn to reach intellectual heights as far above any current human genius as humans are above other primates; to be resistant to disease and impervious to aging; to have unlimited youth and vigor; to exercise control over their own desires, moods, and mental states; to be able to avoid feeling tired, hateful, or irritated about petty things; to have an increased capacity for pleasure, love, artistic appreciation, and serenity; to experience novel states of consciousness that current human brains can't access. It

Philosophical Ethics: Theory And Practice

> seems likely that the simple fact of living an indefinitely long, healthy, active life would take anyone to posthumanity if they went on accumulating memories, skills, and intelligence.(Transhumanist FAQ)

And why would one want these experiences to last forever? Transhumanists answer that they would like to do, think, feel, experience, mature, discover, create, enjoy, and love beyond what one can do in seventy or eighty years. All of us would benefit from the wisdom and love that come with time.

> The conduct of life and the wisdom of the heart are based upon time; in the last quartets of Beethoven, the last words and works of 'old men' like Sophocles and Russell and Shaw, we see glimpses of a maturity and substance, an experience and understanding, a grace and a humanity, that isn't present in children or in teenagers. They attained it because they lived long; because they had time to experience and develop and reflect; time that we might all have. Imagine such individuals—a Benjamin Franklin, a Lincoln, a Newton, a Shakespeare, a Goethe, an Einstein—enriching our world not for a few decades but for centuries. Imagine a world made of such individuals. It would truly be what Arthur C. Clarke called "Childhood's End"—the beginning of the adulthood of humanity. (Transhumanist FAQ)

As for the charge that creating infinitely long life spans tamper with nature, remember that something isn't good or bad because it's natural. Some natural things are bad and some are good; some artificial things are bad and some are good. (Assuming we can even make an intelligible distinction between the natural and the unnatural.) As for the charge that long lives undermine humanity,

Chapter 13 – Death

the key is to be humane, and merely being human doesn't guarantee that you are humane. As for the claim that death is natural, again, that doesn't make it good. Moreover, it was natural to die before the age of thirty for most of human history, so we live unnaturally long lives now by comparison. And few people complain about this. But even if death is natural, so too is the desire for immortality. Yes, people had to accept death when it was inevitable, but now such acceptance impedes progress in eradicating death. Death should be optional.

Additionally, there are important reasons to be suspicious about the anti-immortality arguments—many are made by those who profit from death. For example, if a church sells immortality its business model is threatened by a competitor offering the real thing. Persons no longer need to join an institution if its promise of immortality is actually delivered elsewhere for a comparable cost. Anti-technology arguments may be motivated by self-interest and, as we all know, most people hesitate to believe anything that is inconsistent with how they make money. Just look at the historical opposition to the rise of modern science and the accompanying real miracles it brought. Or to tobacco companies opposition to the evidence linking smoking with cancer, or to the oil companies opposition to the evidence linking burning fossil fuels with global climate change.

A connected reason to be suspicious of the defenders of death is that death is so interwoven into their world-view, that rejecting it would essentially destabilize that world-view, thereby undercutting their psychological stability. If one has invested a lifetime in a world-view in which death and an afterlife are an integral part, a challenge to that world-view will almost always be rejected. The great American philosopher Charles Sanders Pierce captured this point perfectly:

> Doubt is an uneasy and dissatisfied state from which we struggle to free ourselves and pass into the state of belief; while the latter is a calm and satisfactory state which we don't wish to avoid, or to change to a belief in anything else. On the contrary, we cling tenaciously, not merely to believing, but to believing just what we do believe.

The defeat of death completely obliterates most world-views that have supported humans for millennia; no wonder it undermines psychological stability and arouses fierce opposition. Thus monetary and psychological reasons help to explain much opposition to life-extending therapies. Still, people do change their minds. We now no longer accept dying at age thirty and think it a great tragedy when it happens; I argue that our descendants will feel similarly about our dying at eighty. Eighty years may be a relatively long lifespan compared with those of our ancestors, but it may be exceedingly brief when compared to those of our descendants. Our mind children may shed the robotic equivalent of tears at our short and painful lifespan, as we do for the short, difficult lives of our forbearers.

In the end, death eradicates the possibility of complete meaning for individuals; surely that is reason enough to desire immortality for all conscious beings. Still, for those who don't want immortality, they should be free to die. But for those of us that long to live forever, we should free to do so. I want more freedom. I want death to be optional.

Chapter 14 – The Unimaginable Future

Man is a rope stretched between the animal and the Superman — a rope over an abyss. A dangerous crossing, a dangerous wayfaring, a dangerous looking-back, a dangerous trembling and halting. What is great in man is that he is a bridge and not a goal.
~ Friedrich Nietzsche

1. What Would Life Be Like Inside a Computer?

If science and technology defeat death, and if they overcome all other human limitations—psychological, intellectual, moral, physical—then our descendants may live in a world now unimaginable to us. They will resemble us about as much as we do the amino acids from which we sprang.

Of course, I am in no position as a non-scientist to judge the feasibility of, for example, mind uploading; experts have both praised and pilloried its viability. Nor can I judge what it would be like to live within a virtual reality. In fact, I don't even know what it's like to be a dog or another person. And I don't know if I would have subjective experiences inside a computer since we don't even know how the *brain* gives rise to subjective experiences. So I certainly don't know what it would be like to exist as a simulated mind inside a computer or a robotic body. What I do know is that the Oxford philosopher and futurist Nick Bostrom has argued that there is a good chance that we live in a simulation now. And if he's right, then you're having subjective experiences inside a computer simulation as you read this.

But does it make sense to think a mind program could run on something other than a brain? Isn't subjective consciousness rooted in the biological brain? Yes, for the moment our mental software runs on the brain's hardware. But there is no necessary reason that this has to be the case. If I told you a hundred years ago that integrated silicon circuits will someday play chess better than grandmasters, model future climate change, recognize faces and voices, and solve famous mathematical problems, you would be astonished. Today you might reply, "But computers still can't feel emotions or taste a strawberry." And you are right they can't—for now. But what about a thousand years from now? What about ten thousand or a million years from now? Do you really think that in a million years the best minds will run on carbon-based brains?

If you still find it astounding that minds could run on silicon chips, consider how remarkable it's that our minds run on meat! Imagine beings from another planet with cybernetic brains discovering that human brains are made of meat. That we are conscious and communicate by means of our meat brains. *They* would be amazed. They would find this as implausible as many of us do the idea that minds could run on silicon.

The key to understanding how mental software can run on non-biological hardware is to think of mental states not in terms of physical implementation, but in terms of *functions*. Consider for example that one of the functions of the pancreas is to produce insulin which maintains the balance of sugar and salt in the body. It's easy to see that something else could perform this function, say a mechanical or silicon pancreas. Or consider an hourglass or an atomic clock. The function of both is to keep time, yet they do this quite differently.

Analogously, if mental states are identified by their functional role, then they too could be realized on other substrates, as long as the system performs the appropriate functions. In fact, once you have jettisoned the idea that your mind is a ghostly soul or a mysterious, non-physical substance, it's easy to see that your mind

Chapter 14 – The Unimaginable Future

program could run on something besides a brain. It's certainly easy to imagine self-conscious computers or intelligent aliens whose minds run on something other than biological brains. Of course, there's no way for us to know what it would be like to exist without a brain and body, but there's no convincing reason to think one couldn't have subjective experiences without physicality. Perhaps our experiences would be even richer without a brain and body.

2. Would Immortality Be Boring?

We have so far ignored philosophical questions about what we would do in a simulated reality for an indefinitely long time. This is the question recently raised by the prominent Princeton neuroscientist Michael Graziano. He argues that the question isn't whether we will be able to upload our brains into a computer—he says we will—but what will we do with all that time?

I suppose that some may get bored with eternity and prefer annihilation. Some would get bored with the heaven they often say they desire. Some are bored now. So who wants to extend their consciousness so that they can love better and know more? Who wants to live long enough to have experiences that surpass our current ones in unimaginable ways? The answer is ... many of us do. Many of us aren't bored so easily. And if we get bored we can always delete the program.

Many also worry about whether their uploaded mind will be just a copy of their consciousness and not the real thing. But this concern is trivial. When uploading becomes available most won't worry that they are just copying their consciousness. Whether they can upload into a genetically engineered body, a robotic body or to a virtual reality, most will gladly do so rather than die. After all, we are changing every moment and few worry that we are only a

Philosophical Ethics: Theory And Practice

copy of ourselves from ten years ago. We wake up every day as little more than a copy of what we were yesterday and few fret about that.

The situation does differ depending on whether or not the original survives. If the original "you" survives after being copied, then there would be as many "yous" as there are perfect copies. Yet these copies would immediately become different from each other as they proceed into the future. So copying yourself just creates many different people. Of course, there is no good reason to make multiple copies of yourself.

If the uploading process destroys the original "you," then you have transferred your consciousness into as many bodies you choose to transfer it into, although again there is no imperative to copy or transfer yourself into multiple bodies. But the main point is that *there is no important distinction between being copied or transferred*. If you want to preserve your consciousness and have no other options, such metaphysical concerns will be irrelevant. Note also that this problem arises for religious believers who die and hope to wake up in heaven. Is the you that wakes up in heaven just a copy, or have you been transferred there? Again you probably don't worry about this—you just want to wake up!

Now suppose you are facing death with a decrepit body. A new technology promises to upload your memories, experiences, and all your other psychological characteristics to a robotic body, or a virtual reality. Suppose further that the technology has been well-tested and many friends tell you how great it is to exist in robotic bodies or virtual realities. Should you follow them? You may decide you don't trust the technology, or you may decide to die and hope that God or Allah will save you. But if you opt for the high-tech solution, philosophical concerns about whether this new you is a copy or a transfer will not stop you from uploading. Not if you want to live forever.

3. Can "We" Really Live in the Future?

However, maybe this is all wrong. Maybe *we* can't exist in the future. To see this, suppose that we are cryogenically preserved. Even if our descendants revive us there is a chance that our minds will be too primitive to be properly rebooted. Future technologies may be incompatible with our archaic mind files. It would be as if we found an old floppy disk or early telephone, but no longer had the means to run them.

Alternatively, our descendants might reboot our mind files, but find that our restored minds can't deal with their radically different future. In response, our offspring might download their knowledge into our minds, so as to better prepare us for their new world, but find that our memory capacity and processing speed insufficient to deal with the procedure. It might kill us to assimilate all their knowledge. Literally.

To handle all this new experience and information, our progeny could re-engineer our brains or create new ones for us. Either way, it's hard to see how our personal identity survives. Once we have thirty-first-century brains loaded with thirty-first-century knowledge, we are thirty-first-century beings. We would no longer be the twenty-first-century persons we used to be.

To solve this problem our new brains could be engineered so that we have access to our old mind files—thereby preserving something of our personality. But even if we could occasionally enter our old minds, we might find these former experiences so primitive that we wouldn't want to remember them. Why remember being a twenty-first-century hominoid when you can be a godlike thirty-first-century being?

So our futures selves, operating on new brains, would stand in relation to our current selves as we now do to star stuff. We came from the stars, but we aren't stars. At some point, our past lives would be so distant and unfamiliar, that our connection with them would be lost. So maybe *we* can't live in the future. We live, if we live at all, in this reality, at this time. And when that time ends, we do too.

And yet ... we do live in the future ... in a sense. When we imagine it and when we long for it, to some extent we are there. No, our little egos might not be there, that is a triviality best discarded. But as long as minds freely roam space and time we live on—within other minds. This may not be all we want, but it may be all we can get. No one expressed these sentiments as well as Bertrand Russell in his essay "How To Grow Old."

> The best way to overcome it [the fear of death]—so at least it seems to me—is to make your interests gradually wider and more impersonal, until bit by bit the walls of the ego recede, and your life becomes increasingly merged in the universal life. An individual human existence should be like a river: small at first, narrowly contained within its banks, and rushing passionately past rocks and over waterfalls. Gradually the river grows wider, the banks recede, the waters flow more quietly, and in the end, without any visible break, they become merged in the sea, and painlessly lose their individual being. The man who, in old age, can see his life in this way, will not suffer from the fear of death, since the things he cares for will continue. And if, with the decay of vitality, weariness increases, the thought of rest will not be unwelcome. I should wish to die while still at work, knowing that others will carry on what I

can no longer do and content in the thought that what was possible has been done.

So we can make peace with death by accepting this compromised sense of immortality, but if we don't have to die then worries about accepting death evaporate. Russell's advice becomes irrelevant. Yes, worries about how *we* can live on in the future are still with us, but this is always true. The ten or twenty-year-old me doesn't exist now either. But as long as there is continuity between my human self and my transhuman and post-human self, then that is enough to say we survive in the ordinary sense. For what else could it mean to survive?

4. The Overpopulation Objection

Many worry that radical life extension or the elimination of death will lead to overpopulation and ecological destruction. In other words, while it may be best for individuals to live forever, it might be collectively disastrous. Readers may recognize this situation as an instance of the "tragedy of the commons." Acting in their apparent self-interest, individuals destroy a common good. It may be convenient for individuals to pollute the air, earth, and water, but eventually, this is catastrophic for all. However, I don't believe that overpopulation and its attendant problems should give anti-aging research pause. Here are some reasons why.

If we have conquered death, then we may already be post-humans living after the singularity. Such beings may not want to propagate, since achieving a kind of immortality is a major motivation for having children. Such beings may be independent of the physical environment too—their bodies may be impervious to environmental stressors, or they may not have bodies at all. In such cases, concerns about overpopulation would be irrelevant. I am not saying that they *will* be irrelevant; I'm saying that the tragedy of

150,000 people dying every single day—100,000 of them from age-related causes—is a huge price to pay for speculative hypotheses about the future. We shouldn't assume that our concerns as biological beings today will be relevant in the future.

Of course, I don't know how the future will unfold. But preserving the minds that now exist may be a better survival strategy than educating new ones. In the future, we will probably need educated and mature minds—their invaluable knowledge and wisdom. So I argue that we should try to eliminate death, dealing with overpopulation—assuming we even have to—when the time comes. My suggestions may be considered reckless, but remember there is no risk-free way to proceed. Whatever we do, or don't do, has risks. If we cease developing technology we will not be able to prevent the inevitable asteroid strike that will decimate our planet; if we continue to die young we may not develop the intelligence necessary to design better technology. Given these considerations, we shouldn't let hypotheticals about the future deter our research into defeating death.

Note too that this objection to life-extending research could have been leveled at work on the germ theory of disease, or other life-extending research and technology in the past. Don't cure diseases because that will lead to overpopulation! Don't treat sick children because they might survive and have more children! I think most of us are glad we have a germ theory of disease and happy that we treat sick children. Our responsibility is to help people live long, healthy lives, not worry that by doing so other negative consequence might ensue. We are glad that some of our ancestors decided that a twenty-five-year lifespan was insufficient; we are happy that they didn't worry that curing diseases and extending life might have negative consequences.

Chapter 14 – The Unimaginable Future

Most importantly, I believe it's immoral for us to reject anti-aging research and the technologies it will produce, thereby forcing future generations to die involuntarily. After anti-aging technologies are developed, the living should be free to choose to live longer, live forever, or even die young if they want to. But it would be immoral for us not to try to make death optional for them. *If we made decisions for them, we would be imposing our values on them; we would not be respecting their autonomy.* At the moment we tolerate a high death rate to compensate for a high birth rate, but our descendants may not share this value.

To better understand this consider that death is like a bomb strapped to our chest. The bomb is with us from birth and can detonate at any time. If it's in our power to remove that bomb for future generations, then we should. We shouldn't let hypothetical concerns about negative consequences deter our removing those explosives. I'd bet future generations will thank us for removing such bombs, and even if our descendants decide that a hundred years of consciousness is enough, they will probably be thankful that we gave them the option to live longer. I'd guess that higher forms of being and consciousness will want to preserve their being. They would want us to disarm the bomb.

The lovers of death don't want to disarm the bomb because its detonation, they believe, transports you to a better address—from earth to a heavenly paradise where your mind and body are eternally bathed in a salve of peace, love, and joy. That is often their justification for opposing the bomb's removal. The problem is this story is fictional. And we know that most people agree because when humans conquer death when they learn to remove the bomb—they will put this knowledge to use. Those in the future who have the option to live forever will be *eternally* grateful that they have the real thing, instead of the empty promises we now pay for each Sunday in church. Consciousness has come a long way from its beginnings in a primordial soup, but there is so much farther to go. Let's put our childhood behind us, and make something of ourselves.

I will admit that if you believe that humans should accept their fate, that they were specially designed and created by the gods, that the divine plan includes evil and death, and that we shouldn't interfere with the god's plans, then you should condemn transhumanism. However, the chance that all these things are true is small. Moreover, the opposition to the advance of science and technology will not likely succeed. Most don't desire to go back to the middle ages when believers prayed sincerely and then died miserably. Today some still consult faith healers, but the intelligent go to their physicians. Furthermore, everything about technology plays god, and letting nature takes its course means that half the people reading this article—had they not benefitted from modern medicine—would have died from childhood diseases.

Still, there are good reasons to be cautious about designing and using future technologies, as Bill Joy outlined more than a decade ago in his article, "Why The Future Doesn't Need Us." But I reject Joy's suggestion that we relinquish new technologies. Yes, we should be cautious about implementing new technologies, but we shouldn't discard them. Do we really want to turn the clock back a hundred years before computers and modern medicine? Do we really want to freeze technology at its current level? Look before we leap, certainly, but leap we must. If we do nothing, eventually we will die: asteroids will hit the planet, the climate will change irrevocably, bacteria will evolve uncontrollably, and in the far future the sun will burn out. Only advanced technologies give us a chance against such forces.

If we do nothing we will die; if we gain more knowledge and the power that accompanies it, we have a chance. With no risk-free

Chapter 14 – The Unimaginable Future

way to proceed, we should be brave and bold, unafraid to guide our own destiny.

Chapter 15 – The Meaning of Life

All my life I struggled to stretch my mind to the breaking point, until it began to creak, in order to create a great thought which might be able to give a new meaning to life, a new meaning to death, and to console mankind. ~ Nikos Kazantzakis

1. The Search for Meaning

Life is hard. It includes physical pain, mental anguish, poverty, hatred, war, and death. Life's problems are so significant that humans try desperately to alleviate and avoid them. But mere words cannot convey the depth and intensity of the suffering in human life. Consider that persons are starving, imprisoned, tortured, and suffering unimaginably as you read this; that our emotional, moral, physical, and intellectual lives are limited by our genes and environments; that our creative potential is wasted because of unfulfilling or degrading work, unjust incarceration, unimaginable poverty, and limited time; and that our loved ones suffer and die—as do we. Contemplate the horrors of history, and lives so insufferable that death was often welcomed. What kind of life is this that nothingness is often preferable? There is, as Unamuno said, a "tragic sense of life." This idea haunts the intellectually honest and emotionally sensitive individual. Life sometimes seems not worth the trouble.

Of course the above does not describe all of human life or history. There is love, friendship, honor, knowledge, play, beauty, pleasure, creative work, and a thousand other things that make life, at least sometimes, worthwhile, and at other times pure bliss. There are parents caring for their children, people building homes, artists creating beauty, musicians making music, scientists accumulating

Chapter 15 – The Meaning of Life

knowledge, philosophers seeking meaning, and children playing games. There are trees, flowers, mountains, and oceans; there is art, science, literature, and music; there is Rembrandt, Darwin, Shakespeare, and Beethoven. Life sometimes seems too good for words.

Now assuming that we are lucky enough to be born without any of a thousand physical or mental maladies, or into bondage, famine or war, the first problems we confront are how to feed, clothe, and shelter ourselves. Initially, we have no choice but to rely on others to meet our basic needs, but as we mature we are increasingly forced to fulfill these needs on our own. In fact most human effort, both historically and presently, expends itself attempting to meet these basic needs. The structure of a society may aid us in satisfying our needs to differing extents, but no society fulfills them completely, and many erect impediments that make living well nearly impossible. We often fail to meet our basic needs through no fault of our own.

But even if we are born healthy and into a relatively stable environment, even if all our basic needs are met, we still face difficulties. We seek health and vitality, friends and mates, pleasure and happiness. Our desires appear unlimited. And presuming that we fulfill these desires, we still face pressing philosophical concerns: What is real? What can we know? What should we do? What can we hope for? And, most importantly, what is the meaning of life in a world that contains so much suffering and death? This is the central philosophical question of human life. Fortune may shine upon us, but we ultimately suffer and perish. And if all our hopes, plans and loves ultimately vanish, then what does it all mean? This question is not just academic; it penetrates to the core of the human existence.

Given the gravity of our query everyone, if they are lucky enough to have the chance, should think deeply about questions of meaning. And they should be honest in their quest, never cheating like the youths that Kierkegaard described: "There are many people who reach their conclusions about life like schoolboys: they cheat their master by copying the answer out of a book without having worked the sum out for themselves." If we work out the answers for ourselves then perhaps we will find that Rainer Marie Rilke was right when he said: "Live your questions now, and perhaps even without knowing it, you will live along some distant day into your answers."

2. The Question and the Answers

Albert Camus opens his essay "The Myth of Sisyphus" with these haunting lines: "There is but one truly serious philosophical problem, and that is suicide. Judging whether life is or is not worth living amounts to answering the fundamental question of philosophy." Karl Jaspers wrote: "The question of the value and meaning of existence is unlike any other question: man does not seem to become really serious until he faces it." Victor Frankl said: "man's search for meaning is the primary motivation of his life" and "… concern about a meaning of life is the truest expression of the state of being human." And the late, contemporary philosopher Robert Solomon considered the question of life's meaning to be "the ultimate question of philosophy." While major philosophers in the Western tradition have had much to say about the goal or final end of a human life, most have not—until the twentieth century—specifically addressed the question of life's meaning, and many have avoided it altogether.

In the Western world, this lack of concern with the question of the meaning of life was in large part due to the domination of the Christian worldview. During the long period from about the 5th

Chapter 15 – The Meaning of Life

through the 18th century, the question of life's meaning was not especially problematic, since the answer was obvious. That answer was, roughly, that the meaning of life was to know, love, and serve God in this life, and to be with him forever in heaven. According to this view, all the suffering of the world would be redeemed in the afterlife so that the sorrows of the world could be seen to have been worth it in the end when we are united with God. However, with the decline of the influence of this worldview in subsequent centuries, the question of the meaning of life became a more pressing one, as we see beginning with nineteenth-century thinkers such as Nietzsche and Schopenhauer. In the twentieth century the question took on a new urgency and western philosophers have increasingly written on the subject. Thus, with the exception of Schopenhauer, our text will concentrate exclusively on twentieth and twenty-first-century thinkers.

My own view is that the question of life's meaning is the most important philosophical question, and possibly the most important question of any kind. This is not to say that it should be the only thing one thinks about, or that noble things cannot be done or happy lives cannot be lived without thinking about it. In fact one can think too much about it and, in the worst cases, compulsive analysis may lead to or manifest mental illness. Socrates claimed that "the unexamined life is not worth living," but the over-examined life is certainly not worth living either. Life may simply be too short to spend too much of one's life thinking about life. (The Latin "primum vivere deinde philosophare," translates to "First live, later philosophize.") Many persons in all walks of life have lived good and happy lives without thinking deeply about meaning, or without answering the question even if they have thought much about it. In short, philosophers should not overestimate the importance of their ruminations.

Still, such an important question demands some reflection. Without a tentative answer to the question, there seems to be no ultimate justification for any action or even a reason to be at all. To put it somewhat differently: What is the point of living, if you don't know the point of living? Why do anything, if you don't know why you should do anything? You might answer that you live because you have a will to live or a self-preservation instinct; but that merely explains why you do go on, it does not justify why you should go on. Of course, you can certainly remain alive without thinking about these questions, and circumstances force many people to spend their lives trying to survive, leaving little time for philosophical contemplation. But for those with sufficient leisure time, for those that have their basic needs met, do they not have some obligation to think about the meaning of their lives, and by extension the meaning of life in general? Might not such thinking improve their lives and benefit others? If so, then thinking about the question of meaning is certainly worthwhile.

Here is a list of the basic answers to the question of the meaning of life that have been proposed:

1. <u>Negative (nihilistic) answers</u>—life is meaningless;

    Affirmation—it is good that life is meaningless;

    Acceptance—it is bad that life is meaningless, but we accept this;

    Rejection—it is bad that life is meaningless, and we reject this;

2. <u>Agnostic (skeptical) answers</u>—we don't know if life is meaningful;

    The question is unintelligible;

Chapter 15 – The Meaning of Life

The question is intelligible, but we don't know if we can answer it;

3. <u>Positive answers</u>—life is meaningful;

Supernatural (theistic) answers—meaning from transcendent gods;

Natural (non-theistic) answers—meaning created/discovered in natural world

   I. meaning is objective—discovered or found by individuals

   II. meaning is subjective—created or invented by individuals.

3. Cosmic Evolution and the Meaning of Life

A study of cosmic evolution can support the claim that life has become increasingly meaningful, a claim buttressed primarily by the emergence of beings with conscious purposes and meanings. Where there once was no meaning or purpose—in a universe without mind—there is now both meanings and purposes. These meanings have their origin in the matter which coalesced into stars and planets, which in turn supported organisms that evolved bodies with brains and their attributes—behavior, consciousness, personal identity, freedom, value, and meaning. Meaning has emerged during the evolutionary process. It came into being when complexly organized brains, consisting of constitutive parts and the interactive relationships between those parts, intermingled with physical and then cultural environments. This relationship was reciprocal—brains affected biological and cognitive environments which in turn affected those brains. The result of this interaction between organisms and environments was a reality that became, among other things, infused with meaning.

But will meaning continue to emerge as evolution moves forward? Will progressive evolutionary trends persevere to complete or final meaning, or to approaching meaning as a limit? Will the momentum of cognitive development make such progress nearly inevitable? These are different questions—ones which we cannot answer confidently. We could construct an inductive argument, that the past will resemble the future in this regard, but such an argument is not convincing. For who knows what will happen in the future? The human species might bring about its own ruin tomorrow or go extinct due to some biological, geophysical, or astronomical phenomenon. We cannot bridge the gap between what has happened and what will happen. The future is unknown.

All this leads naturally to another question. Is the emergence of meaning a good thing? It is easy enough to say that conscious beings create meaning, but it is altogether different to say that this is a positive development. Before consciousness, no one derived meaning from torturing others, but now they sometimes do. In this case, a new kind of meaning emerged, but few think this is a plus. Although we can establish the emergence of meaning, we cannot establish that this is good.

Still, we fantasize that our scientific knowledge will improve both the quality and quantity of life. We will make ourselves immortal, build ourselves better brains, and transform our moral natures—making life better and more meaningful, perhaps fully meaningful. We will become pilots worthy of steering evolution to fantastic heights, toward creating a heaven on earth or in simulated realities of our design. If meaning and value continue to emerge we will find meaning by partaking in, and hastening along, that very process. As the result of past meanings and as the conduit for the emergence of future ones, we could be the protagonists of a great epic that ascends higher.

Chapter 15 – The Meaning of Life

In our imagination, we exist as links in a golden chain leading onward and upward toward greater levels of being, consciousness, joy, beauty, goodness, and meaning—perhaps even to their apex. As part of such a glorious process, we find meaning instilled into our lives from previously created meaning, and we reciprocate by emanating meaning back into a universe with which we are ultimately one. Evolutionary thought, extended beyond its normal bounds, is an extraordinarily speculative, quasi-religious metaphysics in which a naturalistic heaven appears on the horizon.

Yet, as we ascend these mountains of thought, we are brought back to earth. When we look to the past we see that evolution has produced meaning, but it has also produced pain, fear, genocide, extinction, war, loneliness, anguish, envy, slavery, despair, futility, torture, guilt, depression, alienation, ignorance, torture, inequality, superstition, poverty, heartache, death, and meaninglessness. Surely serious reflection on this misery is sobering. Turning to the future, our optimism must be similarly restrained. Fantasies about where evolution is headed should be tempered, if for no other reason than that our increased powers can be used for evil as well as for our improvement. Our wishes may never be fulfilled.

But this is not all. It is not merely that we cannot know if our splendid speculations are true—which we can not—it is that we have an overwhelmingly strong reason to reject our flights of fancy. And that is that humans are notorious pattern-seekers, story-tellers, and meaning-makers who invariably weave narratives around these patterns and stories to give meaning to their lives. It follows that the patterns of progress we glimpse likely exist only in our minds. There is no face of a man on Mars or of Jesus on grilled cheese sandwiches. If we find patterns of progress in evolution, we are probably victims of simple confirmation bias.

After all, progress is hardly the whole story of evolution, as most species and cultures have gone extinct, a fate that may soon befall us. Furthermore, as this immense universe (or multiverse) is largely incomprehensible to us, with our three and a half pound brains, we should hesitate to substitute an evolutionary-like religion for our frustrated metaphysical longings. We should be more reticent about advancing cosmic visions, and less credulous about believing in them. Our humility should temper our grandiose metaphysical speculations. In short, if reflection on a scientific theory supposedly reveals that our deepest wishes are true, our skeptical alarm bell should go off. We need to be braver than that, for we want to know, not just to believe. In our job as serious seekers of the truth, the credulous need not apply.

Thus we cannot confidently answer all of the questions we posed at the beginning of this essay in the affirmative. We can say that there has been some progress in evolution and that meaning has emerged in the process, but we cannot say these trends will continue or that they were good. And we certainly must guard against speculative metaphysical fantasies, inasmuch as there are good reasons to think we are not special. We don't know that a meaningful eschatology will gradually unfold as we evolve, much less that we could articulate a cosmic vision to describe it. We don't even know if the reality of any grand cosmic vision is possible. We are moving, but we might be moving toward our own extinction, toward universal death, or toward eternal hell. And none of those offer much comfort.

We long to dream but always our skepticism awakens us from our Pollyannaish imaginings. The evolution of the cosmos, our species, and our intelligence gives us some grounds for believing that life might become more meaningful, but not enough to satisfy our longings. For we want to believe that tomorrow will really be better than yesterday. We want to believe that a glorious future

Chapter 15 – The Meaning of Life

awaits but, detached from our romanticism, we know there may be no salvation; there may be no comfort to be found for our harassed souls.

Confronted with such meager prospects and the anguish that accompanies them, we are lost, and the most we can do, once again, is hope. That doesn't give us what we want or need, but it does give us something we don't have to be ashamed of. There is nothing irrational about the kind of hope that is elicited by, and best expressed from, an evolutionary perspective. Julian Huxley, scientist and poet, best conveyed these hopes:

> I turn the handle and the story starts:
> Reel after reel is all astronomy,
> Till life, enkindled in a niche of sky,
> Leaps on the stage to play a million parts.
>
> Life leaves the slime and through the oceans darts;
> She conquers earth, and raises wings to fly;
> Then spirit blooms, and learns how not to die,
> Nesting beyond the grave in others' hearts.
>
> I turn the handle; other men like me
> Have made the film; and now I sit and look
> In quiet, privileged like Divinity
> To read the roaring world as in a book.
> If this thy past, where shall thy future climb,
> O Spirit, built of Elements and Time!

4. The Meaning of Life Explained

<u>The Question and Possible Answers</u> – Answers to the question of the meaning of life come in many varieties, but none of these answers is entirely satisfactory. Let us conclude by considering some of them in turn.

Religious Answers - Supernatural answers are the most popular, but they depend on problematic assumptions about the nature and existence of a supernatural realm. Religious claims may be false. And even if religious claims are true, it isn't clear how a god grounds meaning. For instance, if you are told that you are a part of a god's plan you might ask, how does being a part of some god's plan give my life meaning? Being a part of your parent's or your country's plan doesn't necessarily do that. If you are told that the gods just radiate meaning you might ask, how do they do that? If you can't be the source of your own meaning, how can something else be? If you are told that a gods' love gives your life meaning, you might wonder why the love of people around you can't do that. If you are told that life is meaningful because you will live forever with the gods after you die, you might wonder how that makes life meaningful. You might also question why you would want to live forever with beings responsible for so much evil. So even if there are gods life may still be meaningless.

Philosophical Answers - Turning to philosophical replies to our question, we cannot straightforwardly accept skepticism, since we are forced by constraints of consistency to be skeptical of skepticism. Nihilism haunts us and no amount of philosophizing is palliative in its wake. Yet we reject it too. Why accept such a depressing conclusion when we can't be sure of its truth? Subjectivism provides a more promising philosophical response—we can create limited meaning without accepting religious, agnostic, or nihilistic provisos. The problem is that the meaning created isn't enough. We want more than subjective meaning, and the task of creating our own meaning is enormous. This leads us to consider the objective values and meanings found in the natural world—things like truth, goodness, and beauty. In the meeting of subjective desires and objectively good things, we find the most meaning available to us in this life.

Chapter 15 – The Meaning of Life

<u>Death</u> - Yet this is not enough—because we die. How can anything truly satisfy, even subjective engagement in objectively good things, if all leads to nothingness? Death limits the meaning we can experience since fully meaningful lives necessitate that we live forever. Lives can be meaningful without the proviso of immortality, but they cannot be fully meaningful since they would be limited in quantity. Death puts an end to our meaning and our lives. The defenders of death may claim that death is for the better, but we know in our bones that it is not, as the wailing at funerals reveals.

<u>Transhumanist Answers</u> - Fortunately science and technology may provide our salvation. We might overcome death in the near future using some combination of nanotechnology, genetic engineering, artificial intelligence, and robotics. But this is not enough, for immortality is a necessary but not a sufficient condition for full meaning. Complete meaning requires infinite qualitative goodness as well as an infinite quantity of time. Yet science potentially solves this problem too. If science can overcome death, why can't it infinitely enlarge consciousness? With oceans of time for future innovation, it is plausible to think that science could make fully meaningful lives possible; it could make a heaven on earth. Still, we have no guarantees. Cosmic evolution reveals the emergence of consciousness and meaning, as well as the possibility of their exponential increase, but it doesn't imply that a more meaningful reality will necessarily unfold or that a state of perfect meaning will inevitably ensue. We don't know if science and technology will bring about a utopia or its opposite, or hasten our destruction. And even if a glorious future awaits our descendants, we don't know if we'll be part of it.

<u>Hope</u> - Uncertain that life will ever be completely meaningful, or that we will participate in such meaning if even it does come to pass, we can still hope that our lives are significant, that our

descendants will live more meaningful lives than we do, that our science and technology will save us, and that life will culminate in, or at least approach, complete meaning. These hopes help us to brave the struggle of life, keeping alive the possibility that we will create a better and more meaningful reality. Hope is useful.

The Purpose of Life - The possibility of infinitely long, good, and meaningful lives brings the purpose of our lives into focus. *The purpose of life is to diminish and, if possible, abolish all constraints on our being—intellectual, psychological, physical, and moral—and remake the external world in ways conducive to the emergence of meaning.* This implies embracing our role as protagonists of the cosmic evolutionary epic, working to increase the quantity and quality of knowledge, love, joy, pleasure, beauty, goodness and meaning in the world, while diminishing their opposites. This is the purpose of our lives.

In a concrete way, this implies being better thinkers, friends, lovers, artists, and parents. It means caring for the planet that sustains us and acting in ways that promote the flourishing of all being. Naturally, there are disagreements about what this entails and how we move from theory to practice, but the way forward should become increasingly clear as we achieve higher states of being and consciousness. As we become more intellectually and morally virtuous.

Nonetheless, knowing the purpose of our lives doesn't ensure that they are fully meaningful, for we may collectively fail in our mission to give life more meaning; we may not achieve our purpose. And if we don't fulfill our purpose, then life wasn't fully meaningful. Thus the tentative answer to our question—is life ultimately meaningful—is that we know how life could be ultimately meaningful, but we don't know if it is or will be ultimately meaningful. Life can be judged fully meaningful from an eternal perspective only if we fulfill our purpose by making it better and more meaningful.

Meaning then, like the consciousness and freedom from which it derives, is an emergent property of cosmic evolution—and we find our purpose by playing our small part in aiding its emergence. If we are successful our efforts will culminate in the overcoming of human limitations, and our (post-human) descendants will live fully meaningful lives. If we do achieve our purpose in the far distant future, if a fully meaningful reality comes to fruition, and if somehow we are a part of that meaningful reality, then we could say that our life and all life was, and is, deeply meaningful. In the interim we can find inspiration in the hope that we can succeed.

5. Final Thoughts

I don't know whether life is ultimately meaningful, but I think we have reason to be optimistic; we have reason to hope. And I think *the ultimate ethical imperative is to find meaning in life by overcoming all current human limitations and creating a heaven on earth and eventually throughout the cosmos*. I'll leave the final words about a possible glorious future to Anton Chekhov:

> But at the same time, in reality, what a difference there is between the world today, and what it used to be! And with the passage of more time, some two or three hundred years, say, people will look back at our own times with horror, or with sneering laughter, because all of our present day life will appear so clumsy, and burdensome, extraordinarily inept and strange. Yes, certainly, what a life it will be then, what a life!

www.ingramcontent.com/pod-product-compliance
Lightning Source LLC
Chambersburg PA
CBHW052111300426
44116CB00010B/1621